D1522508

Spiritual Odyssey
Selected Writings of Justin F. Stone
1985-1997

Edited by
Constance Hyde and Jean Katus

Editing Consultation
Lois Mahaney

Good Karma
Fort Yates
1998

GOOD KARMA PUBLISHING, Inc, Publisher
P.O. Box 511
Fort Yates, ND 58538

Printed in the United States of America

First Edition - 1998
Second Printing - 2003

Cover painting - Justin F. Stone

Cover design and layout - Graphic Communications, Inc.
Additional graphics - Spit 'N Image
Text design and layout - Jean Katus

Articles and poetry contained in this volume were previously published in *The Vital Force Journal* and *The New Mexico T'ai Chi Chih® News*, unless credited otherwise. Used with permission.

"Don't Neglect Essence for the Form" previously published in *T'ai Chi Magazine*, February 1990. "Balancing Chi: A Great Secret of Life" previously published in *T'ai Chi Magazine*, June 1988. Used with permission.

T'ai Chi Chih is a U.S. federally registered trademark.

Library of Congress Cataloging-in-Publication Data

Stone, Justin F., 1916-
  Spiritual odyssey : selected writings of Justin F. Stone,
1985-1997 / edited by Constance Hyde and Jean Katus. – 1st ed.
    p. cm.
  ISBN 1-882290-03-8 (alk. paper)
  1. Asia–Religion. 2. Spiritual life. 3. Ch'i kung. I. Hyde,
Constance. II. Katus, Jean. III. Title.
BL1035.S84 1998
291.4–dc21   98-6102
                                                    CIP

Contents

Healing thru Joy!*

REFRAIN
Joy, Joy, Healing thru Joy! Joy, Joy, Healing thru Joy!
Joy in the Heart! Joy in the Mind! Joy in the Soul!
Joy, Joy, Healing thru Joy! Joy, Joy, Healing thru Joy!

STANZA 1
One with all Life, happy am I!
One with all Life, healthy am I!
One with all Life, holy am I!
(repeat refrain)

STANZA 2
One with the Earth, joyous am I!
One with the Sun, joyous am I!
One with the Sky, joyous am I!
(repeat refrain)

STANZA 3
Free as the Breeze, joyous am I!
Free as the Clouds, joyous am I!
Right as the Rain, joyous am I!
(repeat refrain with change in last line) .
Joy, Joy, Healing with Joy!

*Justin F. Stone is an A.S.C.A.P. composer.

1

Justin F. Stone ....

On the next page is a letter from noted Zen writer, Paul Reps, after Justin Stone's visit to him shortly before Reps died. Paul had just read Justin's T'ai Chi Chih textbook for the first time. The letter has been printed as it was written, except for colors that appeared in the original.

Dear dear

in JUST

I AM IMMENSELY ENTHUSED

FROM YOUR GRACIOUS VISIT

THE WORLDS NEED YOU

IT IS EXTREMELY URGENT THAT YOU MOVE

YOU AND THEM

YOU HAVE CAPTURED THE ANCIENT TAI CHI

BRINGING IT RIGHT INTO ANY ORDINARY MOTION

ANYONE CAN DO

    WHAT WE DO MOSTLY

    MOVE

    AND STILL

        FREES US FROM SELF-MADE BINDS

      AND KINDS

KEEPONMOVINGSTILLBRINGING IMMENSEINJOYTOUSALLWITHYOUWITHYOU

Put on Your Think-Cap

Few people think about the deeper aspects of their lives, marvelous though they may be (healing, nourishing, functioning, etc.). Nothing, of course, is more important than Breath. My inner experience is that breath is fire. The beginning of breathing is closely harmonized with the beginning of thought. When one concentrates on a problem, the breathing slows down as the mind becomes one-pointed. This is even more pronounced in deep meditation. As thought becomes one-pointed, and then no-pointed, to the observer breath seems to have stopped. This is why, in coming out of deep immersion, one must consciously reconstruct his or her surroundings, indeed, the world around us (as thought begins again). People who have not experienced this will not understand. If one meditates regularly at home, he or she will have inner experiences.

What part does Bindu play in all this? To me that is the great mystery. "Bindu" has many meanings. It refers to the male semen (the creator of life). In itself Bindu is a point without extension, containing all potential. Perhaps at the end of the Kalpa, when all retreats into latency (with only the Karmas surviving to revive active life), it is Bindu that holds this potential.

Most of us are not suited to inquire into such matters, but to those who are driven to seek the Truth (not realizing that they are, themselves, the Truth), it is irresistible to delve into such matters. I warn against taking literally everything that is read. Scholars have a way of repeating what *they* have read, as, after a while, there is a general acceptance, much in the same way that the victor in wars rewrites the history to suit its own image and purposes. You must go within for answers.

I have never suggested to anyone that he or she "should" do Meditation. If you desire to meditate, I am glad to assist you, but *you* must do the work (practice). On the other hand, I am willing to suggest to anyone that he or she should do T'ai Chi Chih.

Reminiscence

My first day and night in the Himalayas were quite hectic. Contact with a Yogi, who was a friend of mine, led to my agreeing to meet him in Hardwar at noon on such-and-such a day. (Hardwar is a famous spot for Yogis, the location where the fabled Kumbha Mehla is given every twelve years.) Luckily I found someone who would drive me there for a small fee. I had no inclination to ride the old bus; I would have had to balance myself precariously on the roof, hanging on to my baggage and ducking my head each time we came to a tunnel.

When we arrived in the town of Hardwar I asked the driver if he would wait a few minutes while I connected with my friend. Unfortunately, I was unable to do so, though I thought I followed the written directions correctly. He just wasn't there. So I then asked the driver if, for a small additional amount, he would drive me to Laksmanjula, a little way past Rishakish. He agreed.

On the way, there was an incident that left a lasting impression on me. On the way a soft, steady rain began. I was gazing idly through the windshield when I saw a vehicle ahead, a flat cart pulled by a bullock. On the back was a load of what looked like hay, now dripping wet, and on top was standing a beautiful boy of about ten or eleven years of age. He had his arms out as though doing an Indian dance, and he was laughing wildly and, apparently, singing as our car passed the cart. For a moment I felt that I was seeing a youthful Krishna shouting his joy of life, and I looked for the inevitable flute. All too soon we passed, and I was sorry to leave this scene of great ecstasy, spelling out what the Tantrics said, that every cell in the body could be brought to a point of ecstasy.

Reaching the bridge at Laksmanjula, the driver collected his fee and immediately took off. I was alone, but not for long. A group of older men and one youth were eyeing me with curiosity. Thinking I might help, I took a pose as though I was meditating. They looked puzzled, but, finally, the young man nodded and waved to me to follow him. He put one of my two bags on his head, and we took off through the forest. I had hurt my foot in Baroda and it had not healed, so I was limping along, dropping farther and farther behind, when I heard what I took to be thunder. When the young fellow turned around, I motioned to the sky. He shook his head and exclaimed excitedly, "Tiger!" My foot healed quickly after that, and I caught up and stayed close to him.

Finally, we reached a clearing, and I later found this was the entrance to the Ashram. Eventually I found one man, and he spoke English — he was evidently the caretaker of the grounds. He didn't look like a Yogi to me. After he pointed out the small hut where I would stay, he left abruptly. Only then did I find that there was no way to get inside. The door was locked.

As it was continuing to rain, I looked for a place to stay dry. Fortunately, there was a small overhang over the front of the hut, and I huddled under this. There was no way to get anything to eat, so I prepared to spend the night shivering but, hopefully, dry.

In the middle of the night I awakened to hear shouting, then a bugle blowing. By now there was a wild storm going on and the sound of the bugle was eerie and unexpected. Strange noises went on the rest of the night, but it wasn't 'til the next morning that I found out their meaning. Some sort of a constable had come to lead away a Holy Man, who had evidently blown his top from doing advanced Kundalini practice without a teacher. He was smiling and jovial as he

7

Justin F. Stone ....

was led away, his hands bound. I later found he would be taken to a curious clinic (which I would later use one time), not to a jail. It was not unusual for such events to happen. ∎

▼ ▼ ▼ ▼ ▼ ▼

When acknowledging an introduction, Reps would say: "Thank you for your life."

A Personal Opinion

When I was at the Yasodhra Ashram on Kootenay Bay in Canada, everywhere I turned there were signs saying, "Above all try to find God." When it was my turn to head the nightly Satsang, I said, "You're wasting your time; God is not an object." Similarly, when I have seen signs — and heard a teacher — exhorting students to "try harder! work harder!" it has seemed like a contradiction to me. "I must try harder, I must work harder," is an egotistical statement, rooted in the "I," the "small self." To try to be humble is egotistical and reeks of "self-clinging."

Then, how to act? To live in a straightforward manner, to speak in a truthful manner (not as easy as it sounds), is enough. The Prajna, the inherent wisdom that is in all of us, will take care of the rest. To be "straightforward" does not mean to be shrewd, to look for advantages. And it certainly doesn't mean to say, "I want to share" when what is meant is, "I want to profit." There is nothing wrong with wanting to make money, but face the truth, that that is the motive. Hui Neng said: "The straightforward mind is an enlightened mind."

9

Justin F. Stone ....

Out of Bondage

We develop habit energies during our lifetime (called "Vashanas" in Sanskrit), and these not only motivate us in our lives but also make our Karma for the future. We believe we are perfectly free in our decisions and our movements, but, if we study ourselves closely and impartially we will find that we follow certain patterns, sometimes even asking ourselves why we made a particular mistake all over again. When we have found something enjoyable and then find that it is not permanent, we agonize over it — sometimes feeling we cannot do without it. This often leads to actions of anger, which becomes a force greater than our will power. These actions greatly affect our Karma, which in turn leads us around by the nose.

By closely studying ourselves, we may be able to determine our past, or even past lives if we believe in them. An orange tree does not grow apples. The patterns grow steadily stronger and they lead us in a direction we may not really want to go.

For this reason, in disciplines that try to bring us to a state of freedom (as opposed to the bondage many religious organizations aim to impose) the goal is to, in one way or another, weaken these Vashanas and bring about the desired freedom. In Zen it has to do with cleaning out the eighth consciousness (the Alaya Vijnana, or Receptacle of Consciousness). In Yoga (true Yoga) the aim, according to Patanjali, called "the Father of Yoga," is to weaken or suppress the "mental modifications" (Vrittis) which lead to the making of Vashanas. Ultimately, the aim is to go back the way we came and undo the causes, the mental modifications which lead to the Vashanas, which become Samskaras, the tendencies that last through many lifetimes. The Buddha said:

10

All that you are,
all that you ever have been,
and all that you ever will be
is the result of what you have thought.
("thought" meaning the Vrittis that became Vashanas)
If we are not content with our lives, we might take a look
in the direction of these habit patterns. If you really want to,
you can change the direction in which you are heading. ■

▼ ▼ ▼ ▼ ▼ ▼

The telephone answering service (press 3) and the computer
seem to be the new gods, joining the automobile (vehicle of
isolation).

11

Zen Meditation

There seems to be a renaissance of interest in Zen in this country. I am happy that Good Karma has decided to publish my book *Zen Meditation: A Broad View*, which had been out of print for many years. More and more people are beginning to realize that hearing sermons, observing memorized rituals, and believing what has been read have no connection with enlightenment. They are beginning to realize that one must go within and find out Who and What he or she is. This is the aim of Zen practice.

All Zen Patriarchs of the past have stated that the object of Zen practice is to realize one's own nature, "Kensho" in Japanese, and this nature is also called "Buddha Nature," "Mind," etc. Having seen one's own nature, there are no doubts. This makes somewhat dubious the belief of Soto Zen that sitting cross-legged for long periods of time *is* enlightenment. If it were, then most people of India would be enlightened, as they certainly sit cross-legged for long periods of time.

The most famous of Zen teachers, really the seminal teacher of modern Zen, was Hui Neng, the Sixth Patriarch, from whom all schools of Zen have descended. In his famous "Platform Sutra" Hui Neng points out that he never sat cross-legged meditation (Zazen), and felt that long sitting had no benefit for mind while making the body extremely uncomfortable.

In the fifties and sixties so-called "Beat Zen" was popular and very misleading. People began to feel that acting callously was "Zen," ignoring the fact that the Buddha's whole mission was based on compassion. "Compassion" is a word that does not appear on television or in the impersonal media in general. Young people grow up with the idea that the brutal conduct they observe on television is natural to humans. This does not hold out much hope for the growth of a "compassionate society." Our economic life is based on selfishness in the form of heartless competition and this is the opposite of an enlightened point of view. After his great enlightenment experience, Hakuin Zenji declared, "After this, seeing the things of the world was like seeing the back of my own hand." Such a non-dualistic view means that all things are seen as the self, not as hurdles to be ruthlessly surmounted. Jesus' teachings were based on love and compassion; how come they aren't taught any more? Because different people call God by different names, does this mean there are many creators? Zen's view is that we create ourselves in every moment.

D.T. Suzuki said that at the time of enlightenment there is a complete revulsion of the Chi. Turned backward, this would mean that with a total revulsion of the Chi there is Enlightenment. Doesn't T'ai Chi Chih bring about a startling change in the character of the Chi? So T'ai Chi Chih is a means, maybe the best means, to enlightenment.

From November 1991 Special
75th Birthday Issue

*The best advice I can give to anyone who wants to be happy
is: "Just remember that this life is temporary, is transient — so
don't take it too seriously, and certainly don't become attached
to it."*

* * * * *

Flowers on the Hillside—
The First Snow.
Life dies and is renewed again.

* * * * *

Striving, striving, striving—
The years are soon used up.
The brilliant rising sun will set when day is ended.

* * * * *

Evanescence — What is it that remains?

* * * * *

There is rebirth, but no one who is reborn.
Life is constantly renewed, but, as for Justin — who knows?

* * * * *

Walking thru the snow in great peace,
there was no sense of destination.

* * * * *

Trying is not the Way
Not trying is not the Way
You say it must be one or the other,
But I say
Neither Nor

* * * * *

The Soul in (or as) the Breath.
The breath as fire.

* * * * *

Seeing is not seeing,
        lonely the road home!
Off the treadmill,
        brilliant the spring flowers.

* * * * *

Innumerable worlds, strung like
        pearls along a path of daisies.
Listen inwardly;
Hear the wordless song.

15

Justin F. Stone ....

Vairagya: Non-Attachment

To live a family life and be non-attached is very difficult and, at first glance, would seem to be unnatural. What father or mother would not be grief-stricken at the serious illness of a Child? When one is supporting a family, how could one not be concerned about the financial future?

Yet, I have known a few who led successful family and financial lives while fully understanding the impermanence of everything. To feel one's present health and financial status is invulnerable is childish; any thinking person knows these can change in the blink of an eye — or the crash of a car.

The Chinese say, "Make peace with heaven and not with men." This requires an understanding that there is more than what we see, and that all things and beings are interrelated. The English poet, John Donne, referred to this when he said, "Ask not for whom the bell tolls; it tolls for thee." Yet most people are really interested only in the welfare of themselves and their families, the opposite of compassion — not realizing that the welfare of all others is closely integrated with their own welfare. To realize this is the beginning of spirituality. Until all have some idea of this interrelatedness, there will be wars, suffering, and injustice.

When you understand how temporary everything is, racial and religious provincialism will die. Then there will be a better, happier world.

Spiritual Evolution
and the Divine Instrument

There are two histories of mankind: one is cultural, which is lasting, and the other is the study of aggression and violence, which is fleeting. As an example, there are no remnants of the work of the Greek army, but the philosophers and playwrights of Greece contribute much to our everyday life.

The spiritual development of humans is so slow that we take it for granted the egocentric way of thinking is the only one: "How does it affect me and mine?" Both Jesus and Buddha pointed the way to compassion, but that was merely a foretaste. The usual thought is: poor people bring about welfare, and that raises my taxes. No compassion for the poor; they're merely inconvenient.

As one works with the Chi, in T'ai Chi Chih — circulating and balancing the Life Force — the pace of the evolving is greatly stepped up. How we think and act affects this Chi, but, in turn, we are the products of the Chi. Call it the "Divine Instrument" if you want. As we practise* T'ai Chi Chih this Chi will be molded (and accumulated), and our spiritual evolution will be greatly enhanced. We will begin to change, and so will our world.

*Editor's note: The author uses "practise" as a verb and "practice" as a noun.

Energy and Wisdom

Empty space seems to be a vast continuum of Energy, and that energy is Wisdom. Energy appears in many forms, including "matter," and it's always there for us to use in recharging ourselves — hence, T'ai Chi Chih. When we do T'ai Chi Chih our intuition seems to be greatly sharpened, and this is understandable as "Energy" and "Wisdom" are just different words.

Tantra promises that every cell in the body can be brought to a point singing with Joy. Those of us who practise T'ai Chi Chih are doing just that. To become jaded and just *think* of it as "another discipline" is to miss the point. Here are the means; it is up to you to use them.

Notes from Justin

I found two papers I had scribbled a long time ago, saying:

"The soft Kyoto sky will blunt the sharp edges"

and:

"Though I have been unable to detect a purpose to this life, I have enjoyed the quiet of the trees and the sunlight on the water. Should I be fated to return, I would like to work to still the hatred in people's hearts." The preaching of no words, the brilliance of no color.

18

Softness and Continuity

We stress "softness and continuity" in T'ai Chi Chih, and the importance of the former can be seen in the following examples:

The teeth are hard and the tongue is soft, but it is the tongue that outlasts the teeth.
Water is soft and stones are hard, but it is the water that wears away the stones.
Oak is sturdy and stands staunchly against the storm, while bamboo is pliant and bends with the wind. When the storm is over, the inflexible oak has cracked and comes crashing down, but the bamboo snaps back, unhurt.

One cannot strive for "softness;" the very effort of trying to be soft creates tension. It is the absence of any pressure, moving "slow motion in a dream," that allows softness to prevail. The best way to forget worries and ease tensions is to shun the ego-center, so that no one is doing T'ai Chi Chih, but T'ai Chi Chih is doing itself. In this sense, T'ai Chi Chih becomes a meditation.

Identification with the Real

Most people often use the word spiritual (as opposed to physical) without having any idea of the meaning of the word — they just think of something ephemeral. Even if you explain that it means "identification with the Real," they still don't understand because they don't know what is meant by "Real." If it is explained that "Real" means "Lasting" or "Permanent," the mystery remains. Isn't it "Reality" that you have to earn a living and pay the rent? At one level, yes, this is true, but that is not on a permanent level.

India's Yogi Vasistha helped clear away this mystery by counseling, "Ignore the taster and the thing tasted and rest in the tasting only." The taster is subject and the thing tasted is the object; obviously, both will disappear in time.

But the process, the tasting, was never born, so it will never disappear. If this lesson can be digested it is of great help to serious seekers. The one who is just interest in daily activities, completely unaware of their meaning, will, of course, be totally disinterested.

Self-interest is being preoccupied with something temporary. When it is overly strong, it can bring great suffering. Yet psychologists and psychoanalysts deliberately try to strengthen this narcissistic quality.

Properly seen, all happenings are "spiritual," arrows pointing at the Real. This is especially so with so-called "illness," which many advanced teachers look on as purification. We are all spiritual beings.

Prana at Work

One of the hardest things for a beginner to understand is the fact that there must be physical changes for spiritual changes to take place. We are so used to thinking of "spiritual" as being something ephemeral that we cannot at all relate it to the physical organism.

In Krishnamurti's biography, it is stressed that he went through much physical agony, which he well understood. He is quoted as saying, while in great pain, "I know you must do this, but can't you be a bit easier about it?" Obviously he was talking to the Kundalini force, part of all-powerful Prana, responsible for the evolutionary changes, either gradual or rapid. Gopi Krishna, too, went through great suffering, from the time of his awakening until the eventual settling down in his new status.

Prana (or "Chi") is what pulls together the seeming-spiritual and the physical. As we sink deeper into the essence of Prana's action, which we do with regular conscientious practice of T'ai Chi Chih, we become aware of what is happening. To evolve one thousand times faster than "normal" (usual) is no small matter. Some have done most of this in a previous life, as with Rinzai ("Lin Chi" in Chinese). A shy, pietistic seeker when he first came to his master, his personality changed radically (seemingly in a few minutes as he discarded his former identity) and he became an overpowering iconoclast, firm in his "growth of certainty."

Seeming illness, and pain, can point in the direction of massive spiritual changes, something of which doctors do not seem aware. All physical change has to do with spiritual purification and development. ■

21

Within this emptiness is a circle, and within the circle are the mountains and the lakes. There is nothing empty about emptiness!

I like Paul Reps' idea of sitting quietly for five minutes (better make it ten) each day and just allowing yourself to "receive." No thinking, no technique, no mantra repetition, no watching the breath, but just sitting quietly in a chair. In Japan this would be known as "Shikan Taza," or just sitting. The great artisans of the past often did this before starting on some work, such as making a tea bowl or a Samurai sword. In fact, today, many dress in formal style, hat on head, while doing creative work — I have seen them. It is my feeling that ten minutes of quiet and "receiving," plus T'ai Chi Chih practice, may be enough. It is so easy to relax and do nothing, though sitting with the back straight, it may become difficult. We have our worries to agonize over, and, besides, we get fidgety. Therefore it might be good to do it after a little T'ai Chi Chih movement. You may receive more than you bargained for.

The Essence of T'ai Chi Chih

Softness and Continuity are the Essence of T'ai Chi Chih. It is the soft water that wears away the hard rock; the tongue outlasts the teeth. Hardness and confrontation are brittle and destructive; softness and a gentle manner of thinking are life-enriching. The Oriental speaks of the contrast between the oak tree and the bamboo. When a storm comes, the sturdy oak stands solid against the wind until it is overcome and breaks and dies. The bamboo however, bends with the wind and when the storm has passed, snaps back into place unharmed. Softness proves more durable than hardness. Assertiveness takes a back seat to gentle firmness. Overtly the Sage does nothing, and thereby all things are accomplished.

T'ai Chi Chih becomes a way of life. It is true that the gentle movements of T'ai Chi Chih form a moving meditation and an exercise of great efficiency — exercising the inner organs and promoting healing — but eventually it goes beyond these and permeates the life-style of the practitioner. We do not all see the same world, which is a reflection of ourselves. With the accumulation of Chi (Vital Force) through T'ai Chi Chih practice, permanent changes in the metabolism and the thinking process take place and renewed energy conditions the whole way of life. Just as the thought conditions the Vital Force, so does the flow of this Chi, this Intrinsic Energy, condition the way of thinking. As these changes occur we get in touch with ourselves and the world we see begins to change. Joy becomes our natural heritage.

23

I gather chrysanthemums at the Eastern Hedgerow
And silently gaze at the Southern mountains.
The mountain air is beautiful in the sunset.
Overhead the birds, flocking together, return home.

In all this is a real meaning, but
When I try to express it, I get lost in no-words.

This is a graphic picture of a mind at ease, spoken by a contented person. Notice that all allusions are to natural "things;" there is nothing of the artificial. Our way of life is being ruined by the artificiality that leads to a superficial outlook, away from natural "things." Our world glorifies the computer and the airplane, the television set and the telephone. The latter has become our master and few there are who will willing to turn it off.

Culture of discontent
These are all artificial objects which can never lead to a contented frame of mind. And, in our culture (spreading so rapidly throughout the world), all advertising is aimed at creating *dis*content: "Don't be satisfied with what you have, buy something new." In other words, earn money so you can exchange it for objects. Unless you are *discontent* with what you have, you will not rush out to buy and consume. We are thought of as potential consumers. Geography is divided into "markets," population into "demographics," but humans are not statistics; within us lies Divinity.

With all this urge to *dis*content, how can we achieve peace of mind and health and vigor of body? Without these, how much is life worth, no matter what we "own?" Actually, the Sufi master says we only own what we take with us when we dive naked, over the side of a sinking ship! Without going into the deeper aspects of Karma, made by the habit energies of the mind ("Vashanas" in Sanskrit), what do we really "own?" Do we possess the flowers, the evening sky, the soft snow that falls on rich and poor alike, or the seasons that come and go in orderly progression? Do we even control them? These are profound questions that should be studied and the answers can change our attitudes.

How do we counter this urge to "discontent?" In the rush of busy lives it is not easy. Probably we find it too difficult to sit quietly and do sitting meditation; the mind that has been racing all day is not going to suddenly turn off, though breathing exercises will help quiet the mind Ah, but we can move, and find it pleasant to move softly and rhythmically. With the gentle movements of T'ai Chi Chih, even if we do only a few of them repetitively, comes a quieting of the emotions as the Chi (Vital Force) circulates and is then balanced. When the substantial and insubstantial — the Yang Chi and Yin Chi — are brought into balance, we *are* in a relaxed and meditative state. Since this is cumulative, the practice of T'ai Chi Chih in the morning upon arising, or in the afternoon before dinner, or both, can become a very pleasant habit that builds up the Vital Force stored in the bones and below the navel. With this accumulation, we begin to notice the rapid growth of intuition, of creativity and energy, and a strength far different from muscular strength. We may find ourselves moving to the phone before it rings or opening a book to the exact sought-for page. In our work we find a growth of confidence, a belief in ourselves and our center-of-being. In my book *Abandon Hope: The Way to Fulfillment*, I have called this "The Growth of Certainty."

Attitude changes

It always makes me smile when a student — or T'ai Chi Chih teacher — writes that he or she is now much more confident and aggressive in his work, or that he or she doesn't kick the cat and yell at the children from fatigue. Always, they ask: "This doesn't have anything to with T'ai Chi Chih, does it?" To which I reply: "What's the difference, as long as it is happening?" Our attitudes change and we become more like the bamboo, rather than the oak. Then the outer world reflects this inner serenity.

The resentful mind helps create illness. The greedy mind brings war and great discontent. For each frame of mind there is a corresponding Chi. Our thinking cultures our Vital Force. Thus we can influence what we are and what we become by what we think. But, similarly, what we think is greatly conditioned by the Chi, the Vital Force, so our pattern of thinking is not as we might presume, an absolutely free process.

Posture and State of Mind

While teaching "Comparative Meditation" at a southwestern university, a week before practising the Buddha's great "Meditation of the Four Awarenesses" (the "Satipatthana"), I would ask students to do two things during the week:

1) Watch their posture (they would immediately straighten up, though I had not asked them to *correct* the posture), and

2) Frequently, during the day, to watch and ascertain their state of mind. This is not easy to do. At any given moment it is hard to define the state of mind. However, a noisy plane flies low overhead while we are talking and we look up in annoyance; this is "mind with annoyance." We worry about a bill we will have to pay; this is "anxious mind." And so forth.

When students came to the next class, I would ask them if they had practised as requested. "Yes," one would answer, "and I noticed something funny. My state of mind seemed to have a lot to do with my posture, while the posture seemed to affect the state of mind." That person had been successful in realizing the purpose of the assignment. Thinking influences the Chi and Chi influences our thought.

One man I know, manager of a brokerage house, always walks bent over from the waist. Imagine the inner tensions that must present! With such a state of mind, it is hard to see how calm and correct decisions can be made. In India, the hand and finger positions as well as the general posture are known as "mudras." The way we hold our hands can tell a Master much about our state of being. I look at new students' wrists, as well as the pliability of their waists, to determine the amount of inner tension they are bringing to class. As surely as handwriting, which cannot be faked, will tell a graphologist (handwriting expert) much about the character of the writer, so will the body postures paint a clear picture of the inner life of a T'ai Chi Chih student.

When we forget something, we cannot force the mind to remember. The more we try, the less we accomplish. Then, at another moment when we are thinking of something else, a casual association of ideas brings the forgotten something to mind, quickly and effortlessly. This is how the T'ai Chi principle works. When there is effort, tensions result and the meridian channels of the body, through which the Vital Force, Chi, flows, close and the flow is cut off. This is why "softness and continuity" are stressed in T'ai Chi Chih practice. The effortless effort, which we compare to moving "slow motion in a dream," brings results and the energy-giving flow of the Chi proceeds without pause.

27

Softness, effortlessness

How important is this "softness?" There is a famous story of a student and a T'ai Chi Ch'uan Master that provides the answer. Every day the student came to study with the Master and every day, no matter how hard he tried, the Master tersely remarked: "Not soft enough!"

After one disappointing class, the student went home and that night dreamed both of his arms fell off. The next day when he did T'ai Chi Ch'uan at his lesson, the Master finally nodded and remarked: "Now *that's* soft!"

When the effortless flow goes on, first felt in the fingers and fingertips, we become thirsty. The aqueous excess is drying up. This provides efficient weight control (70% of the body weight being composed of fluid) and the ability to lose large amounts of weight (where needed) without any starvation. We are surprised to find that perspiration and fatigue do not have to accompany a weight losing effort. And, at the same time, the *inner* organs are exercised. Constipation is certainly not characteristic of the T'ai Chi way. Many women have been helped with the flow of blood, and one T'ai Chi Chih teacher has given birth twice using the "Around the Platter" rhythmic movement in her home delivery.

We have been concentrating in the soles of the feet to bring the "Heart Fire" down, and as the Chi flows through the body in a downward arc, healing heat flashes may occur in parts of the body, those with blockage. These heat flashes, however, are more apt to occur hours *after* we have brought our hands to our sides in rest. In movement (circular movement), the Yin Chi and Yang Chi separate; then when we come to a position of rest, the Yin and Yang flow together and we become whole. At such time, the feeling is that of having had an internal bath. All this is accomplished softly and without effort.

28

Meridians

What are the meridian channels, through which the Chi flows, and which are used so admirably by Chinese Acupuncture? (We have probably all seen, on television, a Chinese operation being performed painlessly without anesthesia, because of control over the meridian channels and the flow through them.) Belonging to the ancient Yin-Yang science, going back at least 3,000 years, there are many versions and descriptions. This is not surprising when we consider that after only hundreds of years the Latin language has become Spanish, French, and Italian, as well as contributing to English and Portuguese. However, some Chinese authorities claim there are eight main meridians, with the Jen Mo and the Dumo as the most important. These eight channels connect with innumerable minor meridians. There is a meditation where one takes the Chi — purely through the power of thought — through many of these meridians in the legs, the torso and arms. It is too complicated to detail here, but it is efficient in circulating the Chi, as is the Nei Kung discipline (performed lying flat on the back) that I have taught in my *Meditation for Healing/Particular Meditations for Particular Results.* It is through these meridians that Chi, really the Life Force, flows, and many of the meridians have outer openings that lead to the inner organs of the body. This makes possible acupuncture, moxery (conveying heat to selected inner organs), and Chinese self-massage. It is interesting that these inner organs, reached through the meridian channels, correspond to heavenly bodies and to the elements in our world. Thus the Heart is the Great Yang, corresponding to Heaven and the Sun, while the Kidneys are the Great Yin, in correspondence to the Moon and the Earth. This correspondence goes further, into the elements such as iron, wood, fire, etc. with water obviously standing for the Yin

29

and fire representing the Yang. The ancient Chinese Sage knew where the Chi was strongest at certain times of the day, in certain times of the year (Western doctors seem to ignore the seasons of the year completely, though our grandmothers and folk doctors certainly didn't) and a great T'ai Chi system of defense, called "T'ai Chi Gik," was devised through use of this knowledge. In one way, this flow of Chi through the channels is our connection to the Cosmos, just as our breath makes us conscious that there is a power behind and beyond our own will. Incidentally, the Spleen, affected by the aspirated sound "Hu!" in the practice of the Six Healing Sounds in T'ai Chi Chih, is thought to be very important by Eastern doctors, though their Western counterparts feel it is useless and remove it at the slightest provocation. It is very hard for the patient to recover strength after its removal.

Those who practise T'ai Chi Chih do not have to imagine the flow of the Chi through these channels! It is very real, and pretty soon the fingers begin to tremble or other confirmatory signs appear. Since we concentrate on the soles of the feet (the Hsueh, or "Bubbling Spring") while practising, the heat travels down and the fingers may actually become quiet cold while still trembling from the flow of the Vital Force. The inner organs become warm, however, and cold drinks must never be consumed immediately after practice.

Mind-body continuum

Spiritual teachers have always told us that when we find fault with the world, the fault is with ourselves. Zen Master Yunmen, in the answer to a question, brushed it aside and said: "Every day is a good day!" Such a joyous outlook is only possible where the opposing forces, Yin and Yang, are in balance and flowing freely. Ignore the physical functions and it is hard to achieve contentment. The Buddha reminded us that this mind-body continuum is what we must work with. Modern psychology has recognized how much our thought process influences the physical — hence the term " psychosomatic" — though it does not realize how much the physical, the state of the Life Force, influences our pattern of thought. Since thought and the physical are mutually conditioning, there are two ways we can practise our self-culture. We can begin to control the mind and influence the habit patterns, as in Zen or Yogic meditation. Or we can work through the physical, as in T'ai Chi Ch'uan, T'ai Chi Chih, and Hatha Yoga. The latter, however, is a preliminary Yoga and not an end in itself.

Zen practice, the control of the mind, is too difficult for most Westerners. Even in the East, in Japan, Zen practitioners were always few in number, though their influence was great. It seems much easier to work from the physical side, to circulate and balance the Chi, with its attendant effect on the thinking process. To start with the mind is difficult — and often leads to ill health, which I have observed in many Zen monks — while working through the physical, the Vital Force is much easier and joyous to boot. Who says that spirituality must be gloomy and grim? The closer we are to Joy (not pleasure), the nearer we are to Reality, God, or whatever we want to call It. A gloomy, unhealthy Sage would be a contradiction.

If we examine it closely, we find that awareness is the root of T'ai Chi Chih, which is essentially inner-oriented. Circularity is the fundamental. And we already know that "softness and continuity" are the Essence. When we practise T'ai Chi Chih faithfully, we will find that Love Energy is the fruit. ■

31

Justin F. Stone . . . .

No two live in the same world.

Withdrawing into abstraction — from there comes all creativity.

Nothing is in a state of Being; everything is in a state of Becoming (from one point of view). T'ai Chi Chih can greatly influence that path of Becoming.

Posture influences the state of mind and is influenced by it. Just as we can tell the character of a Chinese or Japanese by his or her calligraphy, so can we read people by their posture and the habitual working of the wrists and waist. We can tell much by noting whether someone sits down or falls down and by how one closes a door.

32

Buddha's Answer

The Buddha was asked: "Are you a God?"
"No," was his answer.
"Are you a super man?"
"No."
"Then what are you?"
"I am *awake*!" was the surprising answer.

Buddha meant this literally. Most of us dream our way through life, superficially responding to the Karma brought on by our Vashanas (habit energies). Compulsive behavior is a sign of these.

T'ai Chi Chih Practice Notes

To teach well, it is obviously necessary to *do* T'ai Chi Chih; I know what the practice has done for me. One can't get the benefits without practice. But, whether or not you want to *do* T'ai Chi Chih is entirely up to you. There is nothing wrong in abandoning T'ai Chi Chih practice if you get nothing out of it.

With the coming of the beautiful autumn weather, there is heightening of spirit, a great feeling of "livingness" and, usually, a gratitude for being alive.

As the Zen master, Seigen, said as he was dying, "Better than Zen Doctrine, the Joy of Living."

Zen and T'ai Chi Chih

Two important terms in Japanese Zen are "Mu Ga" and "Mu Shin." The latter means "No Mind," but not in the usual sense. It means the kind of mind that does not react, like a mirror that reflects what comes before it but does not become attached to it. This is somewhat like Patanjali's definition of Yoga: "Doing away with mental modifications" (no Vrittis). It is the true meaning of non-attachment, where no "stains" are left.

"Mu Ga" means, literally, "No Self." The founder of Japanese Zen Buddhism, Dogen Zenji, said, "The way to realize the Self is to forget the Self." Just the opposite of ego-attachment.

The difference between Zen and T'ai Chi Chih is most apparent in the approach. Zen's approach is through the Mind, and has little to do with physical well-being. (Most of the Japanese monks and Masters, from my observation, suffer from stomach trouble.) T'ai Chi Chih approaches through the physical (the Chi), and ends up having a considerable effect on the Mind. Mind and Chi are interacting, each affecting the other.

After one has practised T'ai Chi Chih faithfully for some time, a time is reached where one has the feeling that no one is doing anything, that T'ai Chi Chih is doing T'ai Chi Chih. This is an ecstatic feeling, and it means one has reached the Essence of T'ai Chi Chih. It is actually the stage of Mu Ga, no self. The one practising has gotten the ego center out of the Way, and this is highly spiritual. It is a necessary pre-requisite to an enlightenment experience.

A natural concomitant of this is Mu Shin. (Shin can mean heart, mind, or spirit — the Japanese word "Kokoro" and the

Chinese word "Hsin" mean the "spiritual Mind or Heart," quite different from the physical heart, "Shinzo.") Here the heart- mind-spirit no longer becomes attached, though that does not mean "callous."

Actually, I believe it would be helpful for Zen monks and students to do T'ai Chi Chih regularly. The great teacher, Hakuin, reached his enlightenment after being taught the circulation of the Chi by the old Master, Hakuyu. The circulation and balancing of the Chi have important consequences for those who practise faithfully. ■

▼ ▼ ▼ ▼ ▼ ▼

Spirituality is accordance with Reality. This doesn't come through words or intellectual processes. As the Chi is circulated and balanced, it comes of itself — rather, it is just there. When there is concordance with Impermanence, and you know Who and What you are, it is there.

Flowing Freely

In the Prajna Paramita Sutra, the Buddha speaks of the "Perfection of Wisdom" and the admirable traits of the Bodhisattva.

This Wisdom is, of course, the Prajna, the inherent wisdom that is within all of us. When we let this Wisdom act through us, we are flowing with the Tao, going with the Cosmic Rhythm. The best way I know for doing this is through T'ai Chi Chih, not through words, doctrine, rituals, etc. When the Chi flows freely and is balanced, the Cosmic Rhythm begins to move us, the metabolism tends to change and we become reborn, with great effects on longevity of life.

As to the admirable traits of the Bodhisattva, it is almost impossible to fully express them in modern life. It would mean giving up the "I and Mine," moving away from the "Pleasure-Pain" continuum and ceasing to be selfish individuals, no matter how right that selfishness seems to be. There are few Bodhisattvas in the modern world.

Are we willing to put aside the unimportant to reach this Wisdom, or are we simply interested in entertaining ourselves and being lived by our Vashanas, the habit energies we are unwilling to change or give up?

Why/Why Not?

One time some students from out-of-town came to visit me. After doing some T'ai Chi Chih together, the conversation became more general. As is usual, someone asked about reincarnation (a bad term).

I pointed at the trees in the courtyard. "It is autumn now, so the leaves are falling from the trees," I explained, "but they will be back in the spring. Is that what you mean by reincarnation?"

"Oh, those will be different leaves!" they rushed to point out.

"Why identify with the leaves?" I asked. "Why not identify with the tree?"

That is Love

Your task is not to find someone to believe in or some doctrine in which to take refuge (though this is very comfortable). It is to realize Who and What You are (and I don't mean a name). Then you manifest Who and What you really are; that is Love.

37

Consciousness

People often speak of "higher consciousness." A man is coming from another state to videotape me in a research project to find those in "higher consciousness." The truth is, there is no such thing. There is only consciousness — and, at the deepest level, it is not individual. Sometimes this consciousness is obscured, and then there seems to be "lower" consciousness. It is usually obscured by habit-energies and tendencies; ultimately, this all proceeded from thought and thought-patterns.

The sun remains the same, always, but we speak of "weak sunshine today," or talk of the strong sun in the autumn season. When clouds obscure the sun, we see it as "weak sunshine," but the sun has not changed. Similarly, consciousness remains unchanged but, when obscured by what Orientals call "the dusts," it appears "low." Just as the life essence remains unchanged as there is constant transmutation, so consciousness is not affected by the obscuring elements. One Zen Master spoke of keeping the mirror clean, wiping away the dusts so that the basic nature of the mirror — which reflects unchangingly — will not be affected. Consciousness is like the mirror. It is necessary to remember that consciousness can only exist where there is duality. The polarity of subject-object relationship makes consciousness possible. When we enter deep meditation, where there is only subject and no subject-object relationship, the world disappears. With the reappearance of thought, consciousness and the subject-object relationship reappears, along with self, other, and God.

Future of T'ai Chi Chih

T'ai Chi Chih has begun to spread. Little pockets of enthusiasm have begun to form in isolated places, and these tend to grow rather rapidly. It is exciting to see this. No amount of planning can cause this result; T'ai Chi Chih is spreading and proliferating because of what it is and because of the Teh (Inner Sincerity) of those teaching it.

From the beginning I have felt that the future of T'ai Chi Chih lay not in Madison Avenue or Hollywood, but in the quality and dedication of the teachers. Early on, teachers found how rewarding it is to teach T'ai Chi Chih, to see the joyous, energetic look of students' faces, and to feel the excitement of the group energy. My trust has not been misplaced. The quality of people who have been led to become T'ai Chi Chih teachers is very high. When people come to the annual Teachers' Conferences they find others such as themselves, and the atmosphere is a very positive one.

Active teachers should make a good living from teaching T'ai Chi Chih, providing they stick to it and do not expect instant rewards. Some momentum has to be built, and giving presentations regularly, not just in the beginning, is one of the best ways to build it.

Comment on "Ultimate Truth"

Teachers and students are constantly asking me to write a book on "Ultimate Truth." If I did so, they would resent the very "truth" they asked for, as it would threaten the ground of their previous concepts. This is not what they really want; their desire is for a Truth for human beings, a vastly different matter. And "ultimate truth" is of no value in everyday life. Take the following example:

Nature has no interest in the individual. It oversees the evolution of the species, and the somewhat illusionary individual just happens to be part of that species. Churches promise all sorts of beautiful futures — or hateful rewards — to the individual to gratify the ego sense of importance, and probably, in doing so, they contribute a bit to morality and ethical behavior. But there are trillions of forms of life in billions of universes, and the human intellect is not capable of intuiting them. As heightened awareness leads to an unobstructed consciousness, they can be experienced, and it will then be realized that they are all here now — they are not geographical. When the vibratory rate is stepped up through meditation, T'ai Chi, or heightened awareness seminars, as well as other disciplines, there may well be glimpses of other forms of life undreamed of in the everyday world. It is easy for a higher rate of vibration to be aware of what is below it, but one cannot look up the scale. Greater awareness will bring us to the conclusion that "we" — and all life — consist of a constant flux of energies. The illusion of individuality (maybe this is painful to realize) is replaced by an identity much greater.

Does this mean we now become insignificant dots in one of the innumerable cosmic systems? No, quite the opposite.

When we find out Who and What we are, it is as the Lotus Sutra says:
"Man's voice is a voice filling the Universe, Man's life is a life without limit." ■

▼ ▼ ▼ ▼ ▼ ▼

So often I hear teachers (and students) say, "I can't even remember what I was like before T'ai Chi Chih." It's good you are aware of the change. (I'm sure your friends are.) Sincere practice is rewarded — more than you know.

Presentations

At Teachers' Training Courses the candidates all make presentations. This not done for academic reasons, like doing a thesis for a Ph.D., but for very practical reasons: it gives the new teacher a chance to practise speaking on T'ai Chi Chih to a group, and it also furnishes an opportunity to hear other presentations and get ideas from them.

Once the new teacher has his or her accreditation, it is expected that he or she will get busy scheduling frequent presentations as it is one of the best ways to build classes. Just to sit around and wait for classes to build themselves is foolish. T'ai Chi Chih has a message that almost everyone wants to hear, and good presentations to community centers, nursing homes for aging people, parent-teacher associations, business corporations, etc. will usually receive enthusiastic responses. And, after classes are running smoothly, it is still necessary to keep making presentations as the eight-week courses go by very quickly.

A good presentation should have much personal reference, telling the teacher's own experience with T'ai Chi Chih. This is much more effective than theoretical reference. During the presentation the teachers should get listeners on their feet to do two movements or so in order for them to get the idea that they are not difficult to do, and to feel what it's like to have the Chi flow smoothly. The speaker should have a serene joyous attitude. If he or she performs movements while speaking — which seems a good idea — they should be performed with grace and elegance. Don't make half-hearted motions. Never do the movements of T'ai Chi Chih carelessly.

The presentation must be interesting and get across the idea of "serenity in the midst of activity," something that almost everyone wants these days, when release of tensions is a high priority on busy people's agendas. If the speaker wants to progress to a deeper level in his or her talk, such material can be found in the small pamphlet "Evolution Through Chi," obtainable at no charge.

If the teacher has the conviction that what he or she is saying is interesting, and makes a glowing, enthusiastic appearance, the audience will be won over. Then it is necessary to have definite plans — time and place of contemplated classes — to offer those who want to sign up for lessons.

Just What is Spirituality?

Many books are being written by sociologists, psychologists, etc., in which they glibly speak of "higher consciousness," "Enlightenment," etc., without in the least knowing what they are talking about. It is fashionable to make reference to Eastern concepts and use terms that are just vaguely familiar to readers, usually in Sanskrit. These writers, who have never experienced what they are writing about, seem to feel that greater Social Consciousness and Involvement is synonymous with Spiritual Progress, totally ignoring the examples of Lao Tzu, the Buddha, Ramakrishna and other great spiritual leaders. It is also possible to regard church icons as being the same as spiritual teachers. They often misquote Patanjali, so-called father of Yoga (the Science of Unity, not religion), who plainly said that Yoga is "the suppression of Mental Modifications," the latter being an approximate translation of the Sanskrit term "Vritti." In other words, we have the blind leading the blind.

It is hard to read such books, though people give them to you and ask you to read them. Very often the book, or article, is a thinly disguised sales pitch, giving unknowing people the clichés and quotes that perhaps they crave. Nothing is as saleable as commercialized "spirituality" because people are troubled about life and concerned about death, always from an egocentric standpoint. Recently I started such a book by Swami Rama and a man who calls himself Swami Ajaya. (A Swami is an initiated member of Sanyasa, a complete renunciate.) I was not able to get through it as I am not interested in psychological jargon and worldly "spirituality." It is quite common for publishers to pair a psychologist and a so-called "holy man" with the idea of getting a synthesis of

44

East and West. But Reality knows no East and West and no Past and Future. Some perfectly fine Krishnamurti books have been spoiled by having some psychologist offer his or her concepts of spiritual values, as well as asking Krishnamurti nonsensical questions.

Such terms as "balancing the Aura" or "balancing the Chakras" (whatever that may mean) have become common, and some people charge money to perform these feats.

I define Spirituality as "Identification with the Real." Therapy, no matter how good, has nothing to do with this matter. I leave it up to the reader as to whether the other things talked about (by those who do not know them) and those things practised are "Identification with the Real." ■

▼ ▼ ▼ ▼ ▼ ▼

Spiritual practices are paradoxically an "ego trip." The ego identity is necessarily perpetuated as one's dominant perspective, while the "journey of awakening" persists.

True T'ai Chi Chih Practice

Zuigan was a Zen Master who was famous for the admonitions he gave himself each day, ending with "Don't be misled by others," to which he answered, "Yes sir! Yes sir!" More interesting to me is his comment that, upon experiencing his great enlightenment, he was astonished to find that he was completely dead to himself. That is, he no longer had any interest in the personality called "Zuigan." He might have added that he now saw all others as himself. This reminds one of Hakuin's statement that, "After this, seeing the things of the world is like seeing the back of my own hand."

This is a tremendous realization. In truth, no one has experienced realization; there is simply enlightenment, our original status. This also reminds us of the T'ai Chi Chih experience that "No one is doing T'ai Chi Chih; T'ai Chi Chih is doing T'ai Chi Chih." Do you see the resemblance, and, if so, does it point out the potential for enlightenment in *true* T'ai Chi Chih practice?

It is said that, when Ramakrishna was riding in a horse and buggy, the driver cruelly whipped the horse, and bleeding scars appeared on Ramakrishna's back. To one who is taken with his or her own suffering and with a total preoccupation with self, this is hard to understand. But, John Donne said, "Do not ask for whom the bell tolls; it tolls for thee." Here was a man far along the way in Evolution.

Think about Zuigan's statement. Had he lost something? Or had he gained something of inestimable merit? You be the judge.

Strength of Spirituality

Shambala published a book called *Sword of No Sword* that should be of interest to all teachers. That does not mean I agree with everything in it, but it stresses the strength of spirituality in the type of art we're interested in.

Experts in martial arts disciplines in Japan and China learned how to project Ki (Chi). In *Sword of No Sword*, the warrior Tesshu (who never killed a man) asks a famous swordsman how he remained undefeated. The answer was, "As soon as the challenge was made, I maneuvered close enough to feel the tip of my opponent's blade. If he was holding the sword stiffly, I knew I had him — one swoop and he would be finished. If, on the other hand, the sword was held flexibly with a *steady projection of Ki*, I took no chances — I threw my sword at him and ran. That's how I remained undefeated."

The Kahunas of Hawaii would charge spears with Vital Force before they hurled them in battle.

This should ring true to T'ai Chi Chih teachers, only we watch the wrists and the waist to see if there is tension (and the Chi can't flow) or softness and relaxation.

47

The Physical and the Spiritual in T'ai Chi Chih

Most people who come for T'ai Chi Chih lessons do it for physical reasons, either because of ailments or because they feel it will help them in the areas of energy, hypertension, etc. Thus, they think of T'ai Chi Chih practice as a form of therapy, which it undoubtedly is. However, they may later find that they have derived much deeper — spiritual — benefits, which they did not expect.

How do these come about? How does T'ai Chi Chih affect our Karma?

We are the products of our *Habit Energies* ("Vashana" in Sanskrit), and we in turn have built these Habit Energies. Thus it can be a vicious circle. When these Energies grow too strong they become tendencies ("Samskara" in Sanskrit), and these may last through many lifetimes. These tendencies are some of the reasons people have uncontrollable drinking problems — which they don't understand — explosive temper outbursts, fits of despondency, etc. It is hard to fight against such things when you don't know what you're fighting.

How does all this begin? When there is a release of energy, accompanied by the mental stimulus associated with it, a "Vritti" (Sanskrit) or shallow groove is formed on the brain. Repeated release of the same energy — as when one finds solace in drink and therefore imbibes each time a disappointment is encountered — develops the shallow groove into a deeper Habit Energy. This in turn takes over our lives. If you will introspect, you will find that most of our actions are habitual. We practise piano to develop these Habit Energies so our playing becomes "muscle memory." We learn languages this way. Some actions become so habitual, such as shaving in the morning, that we often don't remember whether we performed them or not.

So we are a product of these Vashanas, which we ourselves built! We are, in a sense, our own creators! We build our own Karma.

I have often spoken of the "Reciprocal Character of Mind and Chi" ("Prana" in Sanskrit). The character of the Chi greatly influences our State of Mind, and our State of Mind greatly influences "our" Chi. How can we break into that circle to change influences for a more desirable effect? We do T'ai Chi Chih, circulating and balancing the Chi. As the Yin-Yang elements are brought into better balance, this not only balances the Chi but it also influences how we think. Ultimately we are what we think; this creates our Karma.

The state of someone's Chi creates "vibes," as we all know. Sometimes we meet someone and get "bad vibes" when that person's Chi is out of balance. We can't explain it — and we often ignore it — but we are reacting to that individual's energy field. Such reactions are usually reliable.

By changing the quality of the Chi (through T'ai Chi Chih practice) we are actually performing the deepest Yoga, going back to the cause and erasing it so the effect will be improved or will disappear. This is, in a sense, "de-hypnotization."

In this respect T'ai Chi Chih has the same deep purpose as Yoga and Zen, but it is a much easier practice. Few are capable of following either Zen or Yogic life to its deepest levels, particularly in our busy society. But we can practise T'ai Chi Chih and have the deepest spiritual effect on ourselves.

Non-Duality (Advaita)

"When the horse in Szechuan catches cold, the cow in Hunan sneezes," say Zen Patriarchs. This means more than the usual statement that we are all somehow connected, each "a spark of the divine flame." It speaks of Essence and Function, the world of particulars within the Void, and the possible expansion to where one encompasses the All. "What is whispered in the ear is heard a thousand miles away," says Mencius, the Chinese philosopher. Thus, integrity is not only desirable, it is vital. T'ai Chi Chih" and "integrity" (Teh), the power of inner sincerity, are one and the same thing. All things proceed from one Reality, which remains the same. The leaves fall to the ground in autumn, but there will be leaves on the tree again in springtime; the root remains the same. Seeing the trees against the sky, we sense a spiritual power.

▼ ▼ ▼ ▼ ▼ ▼

If T'ai Chi Chih is hitched to other activities, no matter how worthy, it will, in time, fade. To use T'ai Chi Chih as the key to open the door to pushing other matters is wrong. Keep them separate. Best to examine motives — at rock bottom level — for this type of activity.

Attitude of Idealism

For T'ai Chi Chih to grow in the future the way it has in the past, it is necessary to maintain an idealistic attitude. I believe teachers should earn good money from sincere teaching — the worker is worthy of his or her hire — but T'ai Chi Chih must not be thought of primarily as a business. Teachers bring something of great value to students — greater than they know — and so many see the changes in their lives as practice leads them to live the T'ai Chi way. This is a great reward for the teacher, who benefits from his or her own practice. In the audio tape ["Justin Stone Speaks on T'ai Chi Chih"] I talk about the effect on Karma, easy to figure out. As T'ai Chi Chih becomes more and more successful, more and more people may be tempted to think of it in the manner of a business endeavor. Keep on offering service; you'll be very successful.

T'ai Chi Chih Community

At the recent very enjoyable Teachers' Conference in Albuquerque [1989], I was pleased to hear frequent reference to the "T'ai Chi Community." I do not take this as an organizational reference — T'ai Chi Chih does not have an organization — but as a description of a spiritual community that has grown very naturally from T'ai Chi Chih. This would include not only the teachers but their sincere students as well. This wave of the T'ai Chi Chih Community is slowly spreading throughout the world, furnishing a constructive force that is badly needed to counter the influence of drugs and violence (all prompted by greed). The peace that emanates from T'ai Chi Chih practice should have a noticeable effect as T'ai Chi Chih continues to spread. It's obvious in the faces of student and teacher alike as they conclude their practice. T'ai Chi Chih is truly a "moving meditation," with spiritual as well as physical benefits.

My most pleasant memory of the conference has to do with the early morning practice, in silence, at the Old Town Plaza — watched by many townspeople — as the sun began to rise over the Sandia mountains. It is interesting to note that the "Sandias" in India are the three periods of the day felt to be most suitable for meditation — sunrise, noon, and midnight. Some would also include dusk in this list.

Don't Neglect Essence for the Form

I have stayed with Yogis, in the Himalayan Foothills, who are masters of *Prana*, the Sanskrit word for Chi. They seem to be impervious to the cold and hunger. Since we ate only once a day, about ten-thirty in the morning (which was not enough for me), one would expect an eagerness to get to meals. However, such was not the case. One time I asked my friend, Maharaj, why he was not at the meal that morning. He replied that he had been meditating.

"When will you eat?" I asked.

"Oh, tomorrow morning, if I'm not in meditation then," he casually replied.

Most of the Yogis bathed in the narrow section of the upper Ganges at about four-thirty a.m., when many other animals were also there. Things went smoothly unless the roar of a tiger was heard, at which the animals scattered and a few monkeys fainted. I have seen the Yogis leave the water, ice-cold at that hour, and not even bother to dry themselves, relying on their inner heat to keep them warm. One newly-arrived Yogi, who had been a lawyer in Bombay before renouncing, tried to do this and became seriously ill; he wasn't ready.

This mastery of Prana and the development of the "Dumo Heat" are the basis of Tibetan Yoga. Some Yogis, deep in Kundalini practice, meditate in water to stay cool while developing this terrific internal warmth. (There is a picture of such a Yogi in one of my books.) I spent two years in developing this internal heat, and the first success was just like turning on a faucet. The overwhelming energy made sleep impossible, but it did not seem to matter. Unfortunately, I was doing this without a teacher and there were some bad

53

side effects, such as internal bleeding. This is all described in my book *Meditation for Healing: Particular Meditations for Particular Results*, with instructions. I would not advise one to practice without instruction.

We have all read how an advanced Tibetan Yogi can melt the snow for many feet around him, just using this inner heat, and I know of a Zen Master in Japan who used to stand under an ice-cold waterfall at midnight, in the dead of winter, to test his discipline and practice keeping the concentration in the T'an T'ien. Neophytes who have tried this have invariably fallen ill.

I mention all this because the circulation of the Chi, and the balancing of the Yin and Yang, are the primary goals of T'ai Chi Ch'uan and T'ai Chi Chih. To just think of these disciplines as exercise is to place them in the same category as aerobics, jazzercise, and so on. Wen Shan Huang spoke of *Chi a Priori* and *Chi a Posteriori*, that is, the Chi with which we came into this life and that we accumulated (and stored) during the lifetime. This is not "our" Chi; we are a product of this Chi. In Chinese Cosmology, from the ineffable Tao comes the Yin Chi and the Yang Chi (the beginning of dualism). This is before there is a Heaven, an Earth, or Man. They are products of the Yin and Yang Chi. To unite with this Chi and to balance it is to return to the "Uncarved Block," and this is what is meant by "Centering." In this sense, T'ai Chi practice becomes meditation.

The ancients have stated that the technique of the form is the least important item, yet we continually hear emphasis only on the outer physical aspects. Contests in combat and tournaments only strengthen this emphasis. How can you look inside the practitioner and see his accordance with Reality? Just as there are Hatha Yogis in India who do incredible things with their bodies, without a shred of spiritual progress, so can emphasis only on the outer keep the student from real fulfillment. Real adepts well understand the relationship between the Mind and Chi. For each state of mind, there is a corresponding character of Chi, and, in turn, each aspect of Chi influences the state of mind. If one will study the Buddha's great "Satipatthana" meditation, or the *Yasenkanna* of Japanese Zen Master Hakuin, one will see how the Chi, the State of Mind, and Spiritual mastery are tied together.

It is my hope that T'ai ‧Chi instruction will not just be physical. T'ai Chi Chih teachers are told that the important thing is "Teh," the power of inner sincerity and integrity.

The Idea of Impermanence

On my recent visit to Albuquerque I gave a talk to over 200 people on the subject "The Spiritual Life" (in a busy world). Many points were similar to the "Merging Sense with Essence" talk I made to teachers at the Minneapolis Conference. This subject seems to hit people hard, as they feel they must get away from family and work routine in order to practice Spirituality (accordance with the Real).

That is far from the truth. I related how a Zen priest in Japan had said to me, "Stone-san, be the *Big* hermit; anybody can be the small hermit." I told them how I suddenly remembered this phrase while meditating with the Yogis in the cold Himalayan foothills, eating once a day, etc. I then thought, "I should be able to do this at 42nd and Broadway!" and left the mountain seclusion the next day. Though I didn't yet know the meaning of "Seijaku" — stillness in the midst of activity — the idea had already begun acting in my consciousness.

In my book, *Abandon Hope!/The Way to Fulfillment*, I have a chapter about "The Growth of Certainty," and once that has been experienced, it is not difficult to sense the Essence at all times, whatever the situation. This usually leads to a feeling of profound gratitude. As Paul Reps says, "How grateful I am with no thing to be grateful for." Note he didn't say, "nothing to be grateful for."

Once we accept the idea of Impermanence, it is not too difficult to experience Who and What we are. This is so well expressed by the Lotus Sutra, which says,"From the State of Emptiness, Man's body is a body filling the Universe, Man's voice is a voice pervading the Universe, Man's life is a Life without Limit."

Three Steps on the Way

In my view, there are three things to be done (realized): To recognize, deeply feel, and accord with Impermanence. Then, and only then, is it possible to find out Who and What we are (transcending Impermanence). Finally, after realizing the above two, to go into the Marketplace and work with people. This is "merging Sense with Essence."

From my standpoint, these are the three steps on the Way. Techniques will vary, but the objectives are the same. And, in these ways, we transcend "Greed, Anger, and Delusion."

Eternity is in this moment.

A Zen Story

A monk asked a great Chinese Ch'an (Zen) Teacher, "Where will you go when you die?"

"Straight to Hell!" was the unexpected answer.

Surprised, the monk pressed on, "Why would you, a great Ch'an teacher, go to Hell?"

"If I didn't go there, who would be there to teach you?" was the Master's reply.

Just One Perfection

So-called "Enlightenment" (different in different traditions) implies realizing Unity. Dualistic thinking or practice cannot hope to realize Unity.

Strangely enough, Mary Baker Eddy seems to have understood that. I do not believe that most followers of Christian Science understand her teaching. If there is just One Perfection, where is there room for illness or hardship? This is from an ultimate standpoint.

To enter the Cosmic Rhythm and flow as this One Perfection is the aim of all true religious disciplines, but certainly not of most institutional religions.

How many are serious enough to profit by what is passed on to them? Most people instinctively divide life into two parts: first, the "reality" of everyday life, such as paying bills and wrestling with problems; then, if there is time, a brief period for spiritual practice. It would be hard for people to realize that both periods merge into one. There is no duality, no dichotomy. Right in the middle of the problems is the time to feel the Essence.

The Vital Principle of "How to Move"

When a student is having difficulty learning the simple T'ai Chi Chih movements, it is often because he or she is not moving correctly and has no clear concept of "how" to move. It is necessary for the teacher to then focus on "how" the student moves, bringing him or her to the point where he or she is flowing in the T'ai Chi Chih manner, not just moving hands and legs.

It is necessary to instruct students that it is "how" you move, not "what" you move that is important. Effortless flow from the Substantial to the Insubstantial and back, is what causes the arms to move softly.

The example the teacher sets for the student is all-important, and, naturally, all teachers are sincere in their efforts to do the best job possible. There are a few excellent teachers who do not immediately begin to teach movements to their students but spend the initial time in inculcating the students with the "feel" of T'ai Chi Chih and the vital principle of "how to move."

So, if you, as teacher, find difficulty with a particular student, you might want to first concentrate on "how" that student moves — always being tolerant and allowing for physical disabilities and advanced age.

The Best Reason to Practise

Karma is an important and frequently-used word, so it is important to understand what it means. In the Sanskrit language, Karma means "action," that and no more. So, when we glibly speak of "our Karma," we really mean the fruit of our action, not the action itself. Even this is not totally correct. The motivation behind our action is what establishes our Karma which is a result and not blind destiny. Usually the motivation that causes us to act is the result of our established Habit Patterns ("Vashanas" in Sanskrit). This is cause and effect. We establish patterns of thought and reaction, and these, formed by ourselves, coerce us into acting in certain ways. So we have created the very force which molds us. Should we not be careful in our thoughts and the habits we create?

There is always a result, neither "good" nor "bad" (which can be seen as "favorable" or "unfavorable" from a personal viewpoint), that is appropriate to the action. When a gun is fired, there is a recoil commensurate with the force of the shot. This adequately explains Karma for us.

People usually believe, not what is logical, but what they want to believe. Thus their actions are rationalized. This has no effect on the inexorable Karma, which is not concerned with sentiment or rationalization.

As one practises T'ai Chi Chih, the quality of the Chi definitely changes. So many say, "I really can't remember what I was like before T'ai Chi Chih." As the Chi is circulated and balanced, habit energies tend to fade and one no longer feels compelled to follow dubious paths of action. One now feels more in control of (and responsible for) his or her actions. This is "burning the Karmic seeds." It is the best reason I know to practice T'ai Chi Chih, aside from the joyful feeling such practice brings. The serenity and better health are the results of this balancing and circulation. And it is so easy to accomplish! ∎

▼ ▼ ▼ ▼ ▼ ▼

It is hard for people to know that the inner and outer are in accord; fundamentally, they are the same thing. What happens in your world is a reflection of the inner world.

Balancing Chi: A Great Secret of Life

T'ai Chi Ch'uan and T'ai Chi Chih, performed properly and on a cumulative basis, tends to circulate and balance the Yin and Yang aspects of the Chi (intrinsic energy or vital force, as some call it). This is one of the great secrets of life, not only bringing healing and energizing effects, but speeding the level of evolution to a high degree. In this respect the two disciplines have great spiritual value and all true lasting healing is spiritual in nature.

I found, in the mountains of India, that these matters are well-known to advanced Yogis. Chi is known as prana in India, and kundalini and shakti are other names for this universal energy.

The great sage, Sri Auribindo, said that if the universe were abolished, this Prana could build a new universe in its place, which is exactly what Indian philosophy says will happen.

All things seen and unseen are really a conflux of moving energies, a reflection of the Tao. When the Yin and Yang aspects are out of balance, there is ill health and worldly events are affected in a negative manner.

We are dealing with a totality here, each event affecting all other events — this is the profound teaching of Hua Yen Buddhism, the Buddhism of Totality.

"When the horse in Szechuan catches cold, the cow in Hunan sneezes," says the Zen teacher. Inner and outer disappear. "Not two," says the Buddhist.

Flowing with the Tao

Chinese cosmology says the first manifestation of life was brought about by the Yin Chi separating from the Yang Chi, long before there was a Heaven (Yang), Earth (Yin), or Man (wedding of the two).

When we begin to circulate and balance the Chi — and there are other disciplines, such as the mental Nei Kung ("Nai Kan" in Japanese) that work toward the same goal — we begin to flow with the Tao.

We note an increase in intuition and creativity. Chronic ailments improve and there is an increase in composure, the feeling of well being.

Professor Wen-Shan Huang, author of *Fundamentals of Tai Chi Ch'uan*, spoke of Chi **a priori** (Chi with which we came into this world), and Chi **a posteriori** (Chi that is accumulated and stored in this lifetime).

If we cease our self-clinging for a moment and look at things on a broader basis, we realize the world (and ourselves) are the products of Chi. We know that electricity is Chi in action, and this intrinsic energy lies dormant in stones and mountainsides.

Everything is throbbing with life, latent and active, so we become one with the totality as we share in the Universal Chi (which really is not individual, though the effects make it seems so). Is this not healing — making whole?

All healing, in the end, is self-healing

Four accredited T'ai Chi Chih teachers are former cancer patients. Examples of T'ai Chi Ch'uan masters teaching well into their nineties are well-known. True healers are using this force, often without really knowing what they are doing.

The Japanese Healing Church, Sekai Kyu Sei Kyo, makes active use of this Chi with little knowledge of it, projecting it for healing effects, first felt as intense heat. Very real benefits result.

Good acupuncturists do not treat symptoms. They stimulate the flow of the Intrinsic Energy and balance it; the results are felt all over. Taking pills to relieve pain or to apparently cure some disorder without trying to affect the cause is somewhat like rolling up a window of the car so the knock in the engine won't be heard.

All healing, in the end, is self-healing. The sincere practice of T'ai Chi Chih, without squabble about different schools and other ego trips, enables us to accumulate, circulate, and store the most valuable of all products (and in some ways, the real one).

Guided by the mind, the Chi comes to life — this is equivalent to safe Kundalini practice. Then we perceive the results and benefits. Only the one drinking the water knows if it's hot or cold. From a healing standpoint, we are not healed; we are made whole.

The Glory of Creation

It has long been apparent to me that everything is vibrant with life. The "empty" space vibrates with energy and intelligence, and, if one gazes at the silent hills and rocks, one will find that they are singing the Glory of Creation. We could call this all a "sea of consciousness," but that would be just a concept. We can only be sure of a "total awareness," and perhaps Past, Present and Future all exist in this fully aware and joyous Now. "Every day's a good day," says Zen Master Yunmen. There is great suffering, to be sure, but who cognizes this suffering? The pain-ridden animal subconsciously hums a hymn to a Creator who is no creation.

One who is aware of Negation of Negation understands that emptiness is empty, too, but it is overflowing with a life that has an insane urge to manifest. And manifestation is Love.

Rapid Growth of T'ai Chi Chih Greatly Surprises Originator

Nobody has been more surprised than the author, the originator of T'ai Chi Chih, by its rapid spread throughout the world since it was first introduced in 1974 at the Open Mind Bookstore in Albuquerque, New Mexico. At that time there was no way of knowing whether there would ever be a second class for beginners, let alone a series of Teacher Training Courses that have accredited worthy teachers numbering more than 1,000. The success of the first class was a surprise, and the rapid spread, by word of mouth and excellent pioneering efforts by the teachers, could not have been foreseen, particularly since there has been no organization, no financial backing, and no hype to convince potential students of the merits of this relatively easy practice.

During the years I was studying — and practising — in the Orient, I often noticed that many who became ascetics and renunciates did not seem suited for that life and remained miserable and torn by inner dissension. In the Himalayan foothills of India, living with the Yogis, I made friends with a man in his fifties who had left his family and renounced the world, a man who had been a successful lawyer in Lucknow and was now following the Scriptures literally in leaving his family, distributing his wealth, and, penniless, breaking all connection with the world. He suffered much from never having seen his grandchildren and, while outwardly a renunciate practising Yoga in stringent conditions, was inwardly torn by all the conflicts of the man of civilization. When walking near the village of Laksmanjula, the former lawyer would sneak away to buy and smoke a cigarette, and then, resuming our walk, we would pretend it had never happened. Where he got the money to buy the one cigarette, I don't know. Later I helped him financially when he was asked to leave the Ashram at which he stayed and wished to make his way, by bus, to Dehra Dun, a place in which quite a few prosperous patrons of Ashrams made their homes.

Such incidents led me to believe that peace was not found by simply detaching oneself physically from familiar scenes. The Vashanas (habit energies) and Samskaras (long-held tendencies) followed one wherever he went; you cannot get away from yourself.

Like Zen, T'ai Chi Chih points out the way to serenity and fulfillment while living in the midst of busy worldly conditions. Advanced T'ai Chi Chih, the most powerful discipline I have come across, is called "Seijaku," which can be translated as "Stillness in the Midst of Activity."

T'ai Chi Chih, working with the principles of the ancient Yin-Yang philosophy, stimulates circulation of the Chi, the so-called Vital Force which is the basic force of Life. We are really the product of this Chi. Sri Auribindo said that, if this universe were to be abolished, this Chi (known as Prana in India) would be capable of building a new universe in its stead! When this Chi is circulated and the positive and negative aspects (the Yin and the Yang) are brought into balance, not only does health improve, but an inner serenity seems to follow naturally. The increased energy (because Chi is energy) brings vast changes in the practitioner's life, both inner *and* outer, if we can judge by past results. At least four of the accredited teachers — all women — are known to be former cancer patients.

T'ai Chi Chih is not a martial art. Not bothering with violence or defense against force it provides the greatest defense, which is inner peace and harmonized Chi. The one who focuses on violence, self-defense, etc. will probably attract violence through the frame of mind. Like attracts like. Can enlightenment, that much misused term, be achieved through sincere practice of T'ai Chi Chih? D. T. Suzuki, the Zen writer, has pointed out that, at the moment of Satori (enlightenment experience) there is a "revulsion of the Chi," a complete change in the character of this Chi energy. Isn't it logical that a gradual change in the character of the Chi energy through sincere practice of T'ai Chi Chih, maybe a half hour a day, then can bring about the experience of Satori?

From the beginning, the emphasis of T'ai Chi Chih has not been on organization (the author has seen, all too often, what happens to spiritual organizations when jealousy and greed enter the picture) nor on financial welfare, though the author does believe the worker is worthy of his or her hire and the teacher worth many times what he or she charges. Many times teachers have proffered checks to the originator, saying they believed they should tithe 15% of their earning to me in appreciation. These checks have always been torn up. Neither I nor any organization has taken one dime from accredited teachers; they keep what they earn.

To enter a Teachers' Training Course, a candidate must have a letter of recommendation from an accredited teacher, testifying that the candidate does the movements well, has the type of character necessary to make a good teacher, practises faithfully, and understands a bit of the philosophic background of T'ai Chi Chih. Then, having entered the intensive course, the student is impressed with the fact that more than technical excellence is needed to be a good teacher. The emphasis is on the "Teh," a Chinese word that can be translated as "the power of inner sincerity." This may seem simplistic, but how can one explain the rapid spread of T'ai

Chi Chih to New Zealand, Switzerland, Mexico, Canada, Chile, etc. without any organized publicity or any organized authority? In a talk I gave at the 1990 Teachers' Conference the deeper aspects of the discipline, its place in evolutionary development and help in developing favorable Karma, thus influencing the future, were stressed. This talk was made available to teachers, on cassette, without any charge.

Our lives cannot be changed by words. If they could, everyone hearing a sermon in church on Sunday, or spending time with a psychoanalyst, would be quickly changed; starting Monday there would be no more cheating or lying in business. But is this so? As the basic energy of life, which flows through us, and, in effect, formed us, changes and is balanced, then change takes place, sometimes very radical change. An ill, depressed woman in her early 70's, not strong enough to take her initial lessons standing up, eight years later is seen dancing in the aisles to music being played. Often people do not remember what they were like before, and do not recall the "troubles" that had bothered them. Remake "your" Chi and you remake yourself. Apparently T'ai Chi Chih can do this quickly and efficiently, and it is easy to learn and easy to do. I firmly believe this, and see the benefits in my own life. Over 80 years of age, this appears to be one of the most energetic and creative periods of my life. So there is much to be grateful for.

The Joy of Life

There are really two Buddhisms. Hinayana (also called "Theravada," or "Way of the Elders") is the old Buddhism that strictly follows the pessimistic teaching of Gautama Buddha. Mahayana, which includes Zen, has a totally different outlook, though still believing in the three truths of Impermanence, Suffering and No Soul or Permanent Identity. The last of these three explains the meaning of "Void" or "Emptiness," which plays such a big part in Buddhism; it means "Void of Self (or Independent) Nature," not lack of anything. The Great Void includes the rivers, mountains, animals, universes, etc. but all these are connected and mutually dependent.

The Buddha and his later disciples characterized this world as a "forest fire" and advised to get out of it. On the other hand, the great Zen Master, Yunmen, emphatically stated, "Every day's a good day." The latter appeals to me more, I must say. If the reader could spend some time in a small, isolated Indian town he or she would see much reason for a hopeless outlook.

Seigan, a Japanese Zen Master, as he was dying, wrote, "The Joy of Life! Better than the Zen Doctrine!" Ah!

Rest in the Essence

Spiritually-minded people follow many paths toward the goal of a one-pointed mind resting in Emptiness (the Fullness of Emptiness). Their problem is that they divide life into two parts: five hours of mundane thought and financial struggle, five minutes of spiritual practice. In other words, they see life as a struggle to make a living, to raise the children, and to let the habit energies drag them around. Then a brief oasis is reached and there is time to briefly contemplate enlightenment (whatever that is).

Such division is not the way. Properly seen, every incident in life points to the unseen Essence. Right in the midst of the turmoil one must rest in the Essence, making the effortless effort while shouting, crying, and feeling bitter and joyous in alternate periods.

In our freedom there are rules we follow, and in our anguish we are still aware of the empty desireless state. To not know, and to know we don't know — that is the real knowing. As my Zen teacher said: "When you once have a day of laughter, then you are on your way." It does not come from sporadic effort.

71

All Things are as They Have Always Been

As soon as we have words we have concepts. No matter how articulate the speaker, how believable the teacher, using words forces the speaker to form concepts in order to convey ideas to others. When one Zen teacher continually counsels his followers to "rest in the unborn," we realize he is speaking from a deep experience, but trying to phrase it so his listeners will understand is a hopeless effort. To him, being "unborn" — and so, "undying" — was real, but, to his followers, it became a concept that they tried to duplicate or imagine. I had a deep experience when it became clear that all things are as they have always been, roughly the same as "unborn," but there seems no way to convey that experience to others. Only the drinker knows if the water is hot or cold.

There are two ways in which such misrepresentation can come about. One way is for someone to have a deep experience and then try to put it into words so he or she can convey it to others. This was the case when Hakuin Zenji, the great Japanese Zen teacher and mystic, after his first great enlightenment experience, said, "After this, seeing things of the world was like seeing the back of my own hand." This is very articulate, but it still doesn't make it possible for the listener to share in the experience.

The other way is for someone to hear or form a concept and then try to have an experience to match that concept. A sincere Christian will have a Christian experience, based on that conditioning, and a Buddhist will see and hear things based on that conditioning. In each case the experience will be the creation of that person's own mind, very subjective, and not something valid that just happened.

72

Those who meditate regularly will probably have experiences that in no way follow what they have been taught. They may then rationalize the experience — and so spoil it — in order to bring it into conformity with what they feel they "should" realize.

Those who do T'ai Chi Chih regularly have not been taught how they should feel or what they should experience. Whatever happens is right and does not have to be adjusted to any doctrine or dogma. It is for this reason that I sometimes do not answer questions which would call for conceptual answers — they would spoil the experience.

To look at a beautiful body of water without relating it to anything is what Krishnamurti called "choiceless awareness," which, while very descriptive, is again a concept. It is better to just experience it.

Words have their place and are absolutely necessary for communication and the accumulation of knowledge, but they are not capable of taking the place of a valid experience. Words are, by their very nature, dualistic, and no realization of "Oneness" (wholeness) can come from subject-object thinking. In short, do not be afraid to experience without labeling, or even remembering, the experience.

Ahimsa and Vairagya
(1993 Conference Talk)

At the fine summer Teachers' Conference I spoke about two requisites for Enlightenment: Ahimsa and Vairagya in Sanskrit.

Ahimsa is easy to understand; it means "non-violence." Of course non-violence goes far beyond lack of physical violence. Envy, jealousy, and cut-throat competition are forms of violence. If we do not have a reverence for all life and a regard for all people we can only spread ill will. There is no such thing as being prejudiced in one direction and open in others. If we love, we spread good will. That is Ahimsa.

More difficult to understand is "Vairagya," meaning "non-attachment" or detachment. This does not mean coldness or indifference. Indeed, the non-attached person is the one most able to act with compassion. With attachment we usually act in self-interest, and that becomes barter. Not to make Vashanas — habit energies — is the way to freedom. When Krishnamurti speaks of "choiceless awareness," this is what he is talking about: to be aware without judgment is his way. "Only cease to pick and choose," is the Zen statement. This is the ideal, but very difficult to follow, particularly when we have family and responsibilities. We should think seriously before taking on obligations, not be forced into them because of our appetites. The greatest attachment is to life itself, the desire to live at all costs and in any condition. The habit energies that have been accumulated through many lifetimes become tendencies (Samskaras), and these lead us around by the nose through life after life.

If the mind is filled with desires that have become habit energies, it is not open to the natural condition of enlightenment. Attachment to self, with the feeling that where we stand is the center of the Universe, leads to suffering, not enlightenment. Then our lives become pursuit of what is pleasurable and avoidance of what is unpleasant, a very narrow view, indeed.

For those concerned with the meaning of life and death, those pursuing "enlightenment," there must be an attenuation of the pleasure principle, leading to gradual dissipation of the habit energies. Then we become like the drinker who knows if the water is hot or cold. ■

▼ ▼ ▼ ▼ ▼ ▼

Acid is Yin and Alkaline is Yang. When the system becomes too Yin (acid), country doctors say that a little apple cider vinegar will help. When I asked Paul Reps how he stayed healthy in India and Mexico (no dysentery), he answered, "I drank a tablespoon of vinegar each day and kept myself hungry."

Freedom

There is great joy when a baby is born and great sorrow when that baby, having become full-grown and aging, dies. Yet every baby that is born will die; we're all dying from the moment we are born. This is not a gloomy statement; it is a statement of facts.

Realizing this, knowing our life and everything in it is impermanent, why do we grieve at what is inevitable? Can we call it "bad luck" that someone dies?

One time the Buddha was approached by a young woman who had just lost her only son. Her grief was great, understandably. She was told that perhaps the Buddha could help her. He listened patiently, then, seemingly in a rather callous manner, said he would not see her that day but she should return the following day. The Buddha suggested that she go to each house in the village and get one grain of rice from each household that had not been touched by death. When she returned the following day, she held out her open hand-which was completely empty. What better lesson of impermanence could there be?

Without realizing (not thinking of) impermanence, we can never find out Who and What we are — and without knowing the latter, ours cannot be a fulfilling life. Without knowledge of impermanence and some inkling of Who and What we are, we are just on a treadmill. We have good times and bad times, enjoy good health and the opposite, and have a few pleasures and a few pains. All this seems to make no sense and resembles the aimless movements of the tumbleweed tossed around in the wind.

The *I Ching* says there is nothing constant but change. To invent myths that seem to give us eternal status hardly helps anything. The cells of our bodies and minds are constantly in a state of flux; this is a fact.

Once we acknowledge that, as we grow older, we will not look the way we formerly did and do not possess skills we previously had, we can let go, "abandon hope," and accept the inevitable, meantime enjoying the freedom from constant striving. Grateful for being alive, enjoying the beauty of each new day, we can be ready to let go when our time has come.

Comments on Newspaper Articles

Recently I read in a newspaper article mailed to me that T'ai Chi Chih is a form of therapy. I also read that it is thousands of years old and was brought to these shores by me. Of course, neither of these statements is true. The purpose of the T'ai Chi Chih movements is to circulate and balance the Vital Force. That this has therapeutic effects is easy to determine. That T'ai Chi Chih is a "moving meditation" which tends to bring serenity and renewed energy is well known. But these are not the aims of T'ai Chi Chih; they are side effects which bring great benefits. When the Yin and Yang are brought into approximate balance (to be perfectly in balance would be to return to the "Uncarved Block," to our "Original Face," a state of perfect bliss) the physical mechanism is in tune and circumstances of life seem to favor us, all subject to the laws of Karma.

People usually begin study of T'ai Chi Chih to correct some physical ailment or to gain renewed energy. We all know how often this happens, and their efforts usually meet with success. But the spiritual benefits, the changes in negative habits and conditions, are more than was originally bargained for. T'ai Chi Chih is not therapy, not exercise, and certainly not a tranquilizer — but it is all of these in profusion as concomitants of the circulation and balancing of the Vital Force (Chi).

As to T'ai Chi Chih's history, I took the original two movements, altered them, and added to them to make up T'ai Chi Chih as it is now. No one had done "Daughter in the Valley" before; no one had performed "Bird Flaps it's Wings." Please don't falsify and say to interviewers that T'ai Chi Chih is a thousand years old, a well-kept court secret.

The great secret in T'ai Chi Chih is what happens to the
Vital Force. We should be grateful for it. ■

▼ ▼ ▼ ▼ ▼ ▼

*Some teachers are willing to debate with students while
knowing full well that the benefits come from the practice of T'ai
Chi Chih, not the words about it. "Why is the right hand in front
of the left hand?" and "Why is this movement named so-and-
so?" — useless questions that merely waste time. Do it and know
that it works.*

Keep T'ai Chi Chih Pure

The task of a T'ai Chi Chih teacher is to teach people how to do T'ai Chi Chih. Period. It is not to ally T'ai Chi Chih with any spiritual or religious movement, which would be fatal to T'ai Chi Chih. It is not to gradually be merged with a religion, a spiritual movement, Reiki, Maharishi's teaching, Yogananda's traditions, etc. — these are completely apart from T'ai Chi Chih. Demonstrating Asanas, speaking about Chakras, showing healing techniques, etc. — all these must not be done at classes or teachers' courses. Asked many times to perform T'ai Chi Ch'uan, I refused. To do so would have just been showing off. As to discussing Tantra — the taking of the solar and lunar forces (Shiva and Shakti) through the Sushumna to the Aperture of Brahma at the top of head, opening the chakras (which are *not* physical centers) on the way, this is a million miles from T'ai Chi Chih and to discuss it at classes or courses would just be showing off. T'ai Chi Chih is complete and most people will shy away from it if these extraneous matters, some against their beliefs, are brought into the picture. If these matters are introduced, T'ai Chi Chih will gradually decline. As to Tantric practice, sometimes called Kundalini Yoga, it is to be doubted that there are authorities in this country capable of teaching it or commenting on it except in the most rudimentary way. There is danger in taking such matters at a superficial level, derived from books or third-hand teaching.

This message is clear: stick to T'ai Chi Chih and do not bring these other matters into contact with it, whether for reasons of personal aggrandizement or to accomplish personal ambitions. T'ai Chi Chih, kept pure, will bring greater benefits than you imagine. ■

Ryoanji is a Kyoto temple that is world-famous for its unusual garden of pebbles and large rocks. Inside its walls one can find a sign that says, "We can protect you from your enemies, but who can protect you from yourself?"

It is easier, of course, to sell Illusion rather than Truth. The truthful person is thought to be either humorous or cantankerous.

81

Universal Energy

There is a wonderful book by Gopi Krishna, called *Higher Consciousness*, that is of immense value. In it he continually talks of "the evolutionary force," the "creative energy" known to him as Prana or Shakti, which are the great instruments in shaping us for the glorious future he foresees. These are synonyms for Chi, with which you are all familiar.

It should be very stimulating to teachers to know that they are passing on the way to tune in to this "Universal Energy," thus helping to shape the brighter future to come. This is not done through words. One can lie on an analyst's couch for years, talking about oneself, and no change or balancing of the Chi will occur. T'ai Chi Chih practice stimulates the creative Kundalini force without going through mental gymnastics; it is direct access to the force the Highest Authority is using to shape the person of the future. Is it any wonder that T'ai Chi Chih people tend to be very creative? Poetry flows, pictures are formed, and the world we know is greatly enhanced.

Practise! Practise!

A T'ai Chi Chih teacher who does not practise himself or herself is somewhat of a fraud. Personal development is necessary before passing it on to students. My teacher from India said, "Before giving water, make sure you have water to give." This does not apply to most T'ai Chi Chih teachers, who practise faithfully.

The Mystery of Myo

These days one hears a lot about "enlightenment." Generally, I believe, it is thought that "enlightenment" is a super-intellectual state where the brain has great knowledge and knows many answers (or concepts). Nothing could be farther from the truth; it has nothing to do with I.Q. rating or knowledge assimilated. When the individual energy (Chi) merges with the Universal Energy (Chi), something acts through one, and that something is infallible. This is Prajna, the Inherent Wisdom. Give it theological terms if you will. Just as my Zen teacher said, "Love is Manifestation," so is "enlightenment" known by this manifesting, not by words, phrases, logic, or dialectics.

In his fine book, *Zen and Japanese Culture*, D. T. Suzuki speaks of Myo, which he says is a hard word to define. "It is a certain artistic quality perceivable not only in works of art but in anything in nature or in life. The sword in the hands of the master swordsman attains this quality when it is not a mere display of technical skill...for Myo is something original and creative growing out of one's 'unconscious.'" (I wish he wouldn't use Western psychological terms.) What he is referring to, of course, is the action propelled by Prajna, not one's discriminating consciousness.

The fencer, the swordsman whose life depends on instantaneous reaction far more rapid than mental response — intuitive sensing, if you will — and the jazz pianist, who has no time to think as he improvises, all cultivate something far beyond necessary technique. It is not enough to be a mere technician, no matter how skilled. When one goes beyond technique, it is Myo, the great mystery. It is the reason enlightened Zen people tend to be artists, poets, etc., all on a spontaneous basis, the manifestation of enlightenment. When I tell T'ai Chi Chih teachers to "Sink into the Essence," this is what I'm referring to — let T'ai Chi Chih do T'ai Chi Chih. ■

▼ ▼ ▼ ▼ ▼ ▼

A day of profound gratitude. When we are grateful we are joyous. Gratitude does not mean rejoicing because some desire has been satisfied.

A Spiritual Discipline

It is necessary to remember that T'ai Chi Chih is a *spiritual* discipline, and must be taught with this in mind. The physical, mental, and psychic benefits can be great, but essentially there is a spiritual power behind T'ai Chi, and the world is becoming acutely aware of the need for such. We wish to urge the teaching always be kept on a high level and that the teacher practice his own self-cultivation so that he will exude this spiritual quality. When it is present, students will be led to a teacher in great and increasing numbers. Good luck!

Teh

The power of Inner Sincerity--
No schemer can find it.
Shrewdness moves in the opposite direction.
Surrender with Gratitude is the way.
Those who seek self-aggrandizement, under
pretense of other things, cannot approach it —
Instead of profit they incur Bad Karma.
T'ai Chi Chih succeeds because of Teh.

Reciprocal Character of Mind
and Prana (Chi)

The reciprocal character of mind and Prana (Chi) means that a certain type of mind or mental activity is invariably accompanied by a Prana of corresponding character, whether transcendental or mundane. For instance, a particular mood, feeling, or thought is always accompanied by a Prana of corresponding character and rhythm, which is reflected in the phenomena of breathing. Thus anger produces not only an inflamed thought-feeling, but also a harsh and accentuated "roughness" of breathing. On the other hand, when there is calm concentration on an intellectual problem, the thought and breathing exhibit a like calmness. When the concentration is deep, as during an effort to solve a subtle problem, unconsciously the breath is held. When one is in a mood of anger, pride, envy, shame, arrogance, love, lust, and so on, this particular "Prana" or "air" can be felt immediately within oneself. In deep samadhi, no thought arises, so there is no perceptible breathing. At the initial moment of enlightenment, when normal consciousness is transformed, the Prana undergoes a revolutionary change. Accordingly, every mood, thought, and feeling, whether simple, subtle, or complex, is accompanied by a corresponding or reciprocal Prana. In the advanced stage of dhyana, the circulation of the blood is slowed down almost to cessation, perceptible breathing also ceases, and the yogi experiences some degree of illumination in a thought-free state of mind. Then not only will a change of consciousness occur, but also a change in the physiological functioning of the body. When the body is mastered (T'ai Chi) the mind is mastered. Master the mind (Zen) and the body is mastered.

Change

The truth is, people don't want to give up their habitual way-of-thinking and responses, even when they know it makes them unhappy. For this reason reformers and missionaries are wasting their time. Though to give people means for evolving, such as T'ai Chi Chih and Meditation, *when they ask for it,* is certainly not a waste. Nothing helps individuals evolve more than these two activities, and as they evolve, their thinking and habit patterns will change.

The Effort of No Effort

Justin shared this comment at a teacher conference: "You can chase your shadow all day and never catch it, but stand still at noon and it will merge with the body — no effort."

Saigo and Daigo — The Vertical and the Horizontal

Some people have a small taste of the Vertical (the unrelieved Absolute) and they then begin to go to lectures, read metaphysical books, and argue with those who don't share their opinions. They have naturally translated their small experience into terms that are familiar with them religiously, philosophically, and psychologically. So they hear the voice of Jesus, or they see Krishna playing the flute, or get a glimpse of the Buddha with two attendants. This disturbs their lives, because they now realize there is something more than their daily experience.

Others may have a complete "vertical" experience, an overwhelming sensation of "oneness" that takes them completely into the Absolute and makes it impossible to get back to their habitual daily lives. They now think transcendentally and find everything in this world tasteless and meaningless. It is very difficult to live on in this fashion, even though the experience itself may have been joyous and almost ecstatic. Many who have this experience of the Absolute are sure they have achieved the final rung on the ladder and make no attempt to understand or integrate their experience. They may become renunciates and shun all worldly life. It is not a happy or fulfilling way to live, however. If they have a good teacher, he will see the dangers and lead them along the way to complete integration, back to the marketplace with all humanity and, indeed, all life. Without a teacher, they may persist in this condition, understanding much of eternity but little of today. They may long for release from this world into a state that they conceive, without realizing that that state represents the state of their own minds. Having escaped

Samsara, and had a real glimpse of Nirvana, they have not reached the point where they perceive that Samsara *is* Nirvana, that there is no need of escape, only integration. They are living in the Vertical, which is steep and slippery and untenable in this world.

Those who have followed a true teacher, or who spontaneously have an experience where they perceive their own enlightenment, are able to make the complete circle and come back to "ordinary" life, which will now appear anything but ordinary. What need for argument when each thing is perceived in itself and seen as being "true?" Such a person has little desire for metaphysical discussion, and no desire to foist his or her views on anyone else. That person no longer perceives his or her experience as "Christian" or "Buddhist," and will get to the point where his or her own enlightenment is forgotten. Not wishing to be a teacher, such a one is a true teacher by example. There is no chance of being hung up on words or written characters. The scriptures no longer serve a purpose as everything in life has become a scripture. Truly, the moon shines clearly in a cloudless sky — yet there is turmoil, joy and suffering, below, and he does not avoid these. The Vertical and the Horizontal have been completely integrated. For how many does this happen?

Balancing the Soil

Tantra says that every cell of the body can be brought to a point of Bliss. If one will do T'ai Chi Chih and then remain quiet for a period of time — not thinking, not planning, not conceptualizing — he or she can experience the same thing. With absolute quiet of the mind, a pulsation will be noticed throughout the body. The movement of the Chi can plainly be felt, and that feeling is one of Bliss.

We tend to cloud the mind with worry, creating problems where none exist. Then we agonize over the problem, completely ignoring the ground from which the problem has sprung. This is "beating the cart instead of the horse" in Zen terms. (Zen is not advocating beating animals!) If the problem goes away, another will arise in its place as long as the ground from which it arose is unchanged.

In T'ai Chi Chih practice, the character of the Chi gradually changes (sometimes instantly), and then the ground where the seed sprouts has undergone a "revulsion," in D.T. Suzuki's terms. We do not fight the problem, be it a lack of something, an addiction, or whatever, but the problem cannot grow in the new, balanced soil. This is the aim of all true spiritual practice, and it happens so easily with T'ai Chi Chih practice, if that practice is regular and sincere. Some people practice sporadically, breaking off practice whenever there is something to worry over or resent, thus taking away the very tool which could be a help!

Constant resentment should be a warning to a person that something is wrong; the soil is ripe for new planting. Resentment comes from self-clinging. "Who are you to tell me what to do?" we say, creating a problem where none existed. Take a good look at the ground from which the resentment or the problem arose. Have the habit energies, the attachments, created that ground?■

▼ ▼ ▼ ▼ ▼ ▼

It is written that the great Sufi Teacher, Sheik Abdullah Ansari, said:

> *What is worship?*
> *To realize reality.*
> *What is the sacred law?*
> *To do no evil.*
> *What is reality?*
> *Selflessness.*

This is right on; nothing need be added. Those who faithfully practise T'ai Chi Chih move rapidly toward identity with reality. This is the real "evolution."

T'ai Chi Chih and Non-Duality

"Advaita" in Sanskrit means "Non-Duality." This is a difficult concept for most people as we look about us and see multiple objects. But what we see are only transformations, not permanent forms, whether we are speaking of a chair, a tree, or a human being. Each exists provisionally, but is certainly not lasting. One day the tree may become the chair and the human body will be eaten by worms. The "I" that observes all this may disappear and become another "I." To bank on permanence is to promote suffering.

When we perform T'ai Chi Chih properly we feel the results. Since we are, essentially a conflux of moving energies, stimulating and balancing the Intrinsic Energy (Chi) affects our whole being. The effects seem to be personal, but, in truth, they are widespread. Just as our Enlightenment *is* "Saving All Beings," so does the balancing of the Universal Energy affect both the outer and the inner. So many students have written me about how their lives have changed with the practice of T'ai Chi Chih!

Those who truly practise note that their attitudes change — and others notice it, too. We do not heal symptoms; we become "whole." So, to practise regularly and sincerely is to promote the positive in this world; we reap the benefits. This is "Advaita" in action.

Anger: A Choice

Anger usually comes from preoccupation with self. This other one has injured this self so precious to me, insulted or denigrated this ego that is separate from all others. Spiritually-minded people feel a common identity with others, so they do not give way easily to anger. Meditation — and T'ai Chi Chih — tranquilize the mind without dulling it.

To those quick to anger, I would suggest sleeping on it before countering in any way. Once anger — and sometimes violence — is vented on another, it is too late to recall it. Ahimsa means non-injury in thought, action and intent. To act differently is to dig the deep pit of Karma; we make our own future.

T'ai Chi Chih is softness in action, like the bamboo that bends gracefully before the wind but does not break. No one is doing it; T'ai Chi Chih is doing T'ai Chi Chih. There is a timeless moment as we flow effortlessly through very heavy air.

At the risk of sounding "preachy," let me say: Be honest with yourself. Don't rationalize. Do you find your actions accord with your words — honestly? If you find out who and what you are, they certainly will. But your motive and ambitions may get in your way. Don't judge them; just recognize them for what they are. That is enough. Ah, a world without anger!

Enlightenment

One Zen Master told his disciples that, after they have experienced Enlightenment, they should forget it as it is of absolutely no use in life. This is misleading to those inexperienced ones who read it. After a true Enlightenment experience, one is never the same, even though he or she consciously forgets the joy and fulfillment and goes on to work for others. In Zen practice, particularly in Rinzai Zen (which uses the Koan practice), it is possible to force a premature Satori experience through overly-zealous practice, and the results of the experience will soon fade. This is the danger of this kind of practice. Better is the slow maturing that leads to the "instantaneous" Satori. It is possible to have many Satori experiences in a lifetime. Hakuin, one of Japan's two greatest teachers, reports having had quite a few of the "great joys" and innumerable smaller experiences. This reminds us of Ramakrishna, the Indian Saint who, in his mature years, was often in a perpetual state corresponding to Satori, to the extent that he was unconscious of the everyday world for long periods of time. Such a state would be misunderstood in the West, where doctors might diagnose it as hysteria.

Zen says that you must leave each state as it is experienced, as a cloud floats across the sky, stopping at no one place. For complete non-attachment, nothing should be clung to, even Enlightenment. And this term, Enlightenment, is used differently in different cultures. As I have pointed out before, the Enlightenment of the great Rishi in India was far different from the Buddhist Enlightenment in China and Japan.

It is possible to mistake a conceptual state, in which things are supposedly understood, for a genuine Enlightenment experience, where "understanding" is the least of the concerns.

Experiencing something, living something, manifesting it, is far different from having an intellectual understanding. Words play no part in the genuine article, and the realization of this Unity often leaves one tongue-tied. In Zen terms, Enlightenment is chopping wood and drawing water. Those who look for the miraculous or the showy are up the wrong creek. My Indian teacher said that only an Enlightened person (perhaps the teacher) could tell you of *your* Enlightenment. If someone says, "I'm enlightened!" you can be sure he or she is a million miles away. Only the teacher, or one like the teacher, can confirm the student's status. His or her words of having gone past the teacher would give the student away.

There is Reality in the events of the world, particularly those having to do with nature. The trick is in the eye of the beholder.

Flow Slow Motion

Teachers should remember that the most important thing with beginning students is to see that they move correctly. Once they learn how to *flow* slow motion in a dream, there is no problem in teaching them the movements. I hope teachers keep this in mind and concentrate, in the beginning, on getting the students to flow with softness and continuity. ■

▼ ▼ ▼ ▼ ▼ ▼

Some T'ai Chi Chih teachers are doing well financially, and I am all for it. The worker is always worthy of his or her hire. But do not be an opportunist. Hypocrisy is one way to be popular, but it is better to bring your words and your actions together, so that they say the same thing.

A Common Problem

Zen books are popular reading, and bookstores are full of new ones constantly coming out. These are usually written by scholars, psychologists, etc, who have not practised or have not realized anything. They take standard works of Zen, such as the *Mumonkan* or *Hekiganyoku*, that have well-known "cases" — dialogues or commentaries on historical incidents — and rewrite them or state them and then give commentaries. Sometimes the writers are merely translators, without the Buddhist knowledge or experience to know what the words mean, and words change meaning according to context. For instance, how can you define the word "spring" without knowing the context in which it is used?

Readers of these books, nibbling the delicious candy, fail to realize that the "cases" being cited, and the talks being quoted, were all formed for the benefit of monks — renunciates who are devoting their entire lives to Zen practice. Then the readers try to apply the lessons to themselves, who may be professionals with children and loving wives or husbands. Are they supposed to strip their lives of love and joy to fulfill an ideal stated in a book for monks? It would be impossible and not at all advisable.

The Cumulative Effects of T'ai Chi Chih

With regularity of practice, the deeper meanings of T'ai Chi Chih become evident after some time. If one does not practise regularly, it is like a pianist who does finger exercises once every two weeks, or an athlete who eats only intermittently; there is no real nourishment.

As people learn T'ai Chi Chih, they become attracted to it because of the way they feel. Some then want to go on and become teachers, passing along the good feeling and enjoying the reactions of their classes. Early on there is great enthusiasm: so why do people drop away from practice?

In our society there is a great restlessness, a desire for diversity and titillation. Even when something is going well and satisfaction is being attained, there is a desire to look far afield and seek something else. The far-off fields may look greener, but more is not better. If a chela (disciple) is told by his or her guru to follow a certain discipline, the chela does it faithfully. This may go on for years. If a potential opera singer wants to really polish his or her talents, it is necessary to make great effort. Ballet dancers are famous for being up early the morning after a performance, even a triumphant one, working at the bar in the practice room. Such motivation is necessary to make a successful performing artist. The point is that T'ai Chi Chih results are cumulative. Regular practice leads to the Chi firming the bones, and the Chi is progressively stored in the T'an T'ien. The changes in personality then often become remarkable, as the evolving power of the circulated and balanced Chi takes hold. One can literally remake him or herself — if there is the sticking power.

All teachers, of course, must practice regularly so that they are led by an inner wisdom (Prajna). T'ai Chi Chih skills develop with practice, and it is easy for the experienced teacher to tell who is practicing by watching the performance. (Others, more experienced, can tell just by looking at the teacher.)

If you will remember that T'ai Chi Chih benefits are cumulative, and that, in my opinion, the circulation and balancing of the Chi (Prana) is the most important of activities, perhaps you will be motivated to practise regularly, and even step up the length of time that you practise. It is well worth the effort, because the rewards are great. ■

▼ ▼ ▼ ▼ ▼ ▼

Holy and unholy: Is there anything that is not holy? Isn't every rock and blade of grass sacred? Can't holy and unholy be manipulated, as Krishnamurti suggests? From one point of view, each word is the word of God; every happening points to Reality. Seen this way, what is unholy? Bad Karma? Bodhidharma answered the Chinese Emperor, who asked for the "Holy Truth," "Vast emptiness and nothing holy about it." The term "Vast Emptiness" is hard for most to comprehend, but that is another matter.

A Look at T'ai Chi Chih and Illness

When a prospective student of T'ai Chi Chih asks, "Will it help my arthritis?" the answer should be something like this, "Why don't you try it and see? You may find benefits you didn't expect." Under no circumstance should the teacher answer "Yes!" It would be possible to describe how a certain specific person had been helped, which promises nothing. For instance, a teacher once wrote how he went from 255 pounds to 180 pounds. That's not opinion; it's a case history. But we would never want to infer that T'ai Chi Chih is a specific for ANY disease or ailment. It is possible to say that the circulation and balancing of the Chi have helped many people. To the right person (only), it could be said that T'ai Chi Chih practice has wide spiritual effects, but not everybody would understand that. From my personal standpoint, all so-called illness is a spiritual purification, and there is a purpose to it in both our physical and spiritual evolution. However, it is not necessary to hold out a carrot to a potential student: the practice of T'ai Chi Chih is joyous, it's fun. Being easy, and easily learned, it's not hard to persuade others to want to do it. I believe everybody is a potential candidate for T'ai Chi Chih. Am I prejudiced? Yes!

To Cling or Not to Cling

"You've been on the Spiritual Path for 40 years. What have you learned?"

"I've learned that there is nothing to be done."

"Ah, but if you hadn't been on the Path for 40 years, you wouldn't know there's nothing to be done!"

It is hard to convince earnest students that it's all there, inside, and nothing has to be learned or accumulated. Being earnest, we want to make a special effort, and that effort can be self-defeating. Once the habit energies are put aside, only Wisdom shines through, but the habit energies and tendencies that develop from them cover the Inherent Wisdom.

Clinging to the habit energies (an addiction hard to break) is self-clinging. The Buddha said that suffering is caused by self-clinging, which causes greed, anger and delusion. Look at your troubles and decide if they, ultimately, aren't caused by over-concern with self. We can't see the forest if we concentrate on one tree. When people write me of their problems, I usually note that all the sentences begin with "I."

Dwelling on the past, easy to do, is self-clinging. Living in the present, with gratitude, is rare. When we know Who and What we are, it is not difficult.

Aesthetics and Spirituality

The truly spiritual person is apt to be aesthetically advanced. As it says in the Buddhist *Abidhamma*, "In the contemplation of the beautiful, there are no selfish motives and man is free from the ego." The complete absence of the ego, if maintained, is Nirvana.

At times, I have been puzzled by the absence of aesthetic perception on the part of some seemingly spiritual people, and very often I have been subsequently disappointed by them. The superficial spirituality is the result of the stirring of the Kundalini — a physical basis, not an inherent tendency — and this may also cause an unusually strong attraction toward great sexual activity. Conversely, the seemingly erotic-minded person very often carries the seed of great spirituality. Heightening of the Prana (Chi) certainly can strengthen the libidinous tendencies as well as strengthening the evolutionary spiritual progress.

Human-Heartedness

Buddhism stresses that "things causally produced are void," that is, temporary and not enduring. Lao Tzu's Taoism speaks of "not attempting to play the Tao, letting the Tao play you." Hinduism, and there are numerous kinds of Hinduism, counsels faith in numerous gods, all emanations of the one Deity (or Reality). These all have deep roots, too difficult to understand intellectually. However, Confucius' Teaching of "Human-Heartedness" as being most important, is easy to understand and quick to ring a bell. He felt that Human-Heartedness, along with "Teh" (the power of inner sincerity) was most important. As my late friend, Swami Krishnanand, stressed, "If you don't find God in the hearts of men, where do you expect to find Him?" Cheating another person, cutting corners to get a slight monetary advantage, is the opposite of "human-heartedness." The fact that you can get away with it has nothing to do with it. It's good to examine your financial actions in light of Teh and Human-Heartedness. And, above all, it's necessary to be honest with yourself and not rationalize.

103

Meditation and Transformation

In forty-three years of following a spiritual path, what has always amazed me is that my own inner experience has very seldom coincided with the written and spoken teaching I had been exposed to. There have been exceptions. When I first read *The Buddhism of Totality* by Garma C.C. Chang, the teachings of esoteric Hua-Yen Buddhism, I found an exact description of what I had known — but never heard — for many, many years. Meditation will often take one to a "higher" level of vibration, in which case numerous other universes may be experienced. These will not in any way resemble this universe, which scientists mistakenly, and chauvinistically, hold to be the only one. Experiencing these, it is not known if what is seen (interconnecting shafts of light, etc.) are even creatures. Other universes described in some Buddhism, which I presume the Buddha experienced, have strange descriptions of places where there is "neither thought nor no-thought" or "neither form nor no-form," entirely beyond our ability to comprehend. Such sights, of course, tear to shreds conventional church views, and so would not be admissible even if experienced. Little theology is based on experience; most on theory and blind faith. When asked about such experiences, my Indian teacher would answer, "Why should you doubt your own experience?"

That some energy, possibly combined with wisdom, comes "down from above" hardly fits my preconceived notions (being an iconoclast) but, nevertheless, I have seen and felt it. T'ai Chi Chih practice, if coupled with meditation, will strengthen the possibilities of such experience, but, if you are a devout church believer, it would be unlikely that you could go beyond your own religious conditioning.

The devout Bhakti is said to go into ecstasy at the creaking of a water wheel. Read Kabir's poetry. On the other hand, the Jnani is following the way of inquiry, to separate the "real" from the "unreal." In my view there is no "unreal," only transformation. What is alive stays alive, only it changes. And my own experience has been, "Everything is singing the Glory of Creation."■

▼ ▼ ▼ ▼ ▼ ▼

The Real within the apparent (Host within the Guest) — this is the Great Mystery.

A Great Bonus

Zen practice, no matter what you hear, is aimed at having you realize your own true nature. When you suddenly find out Who and What you are, it is a big surprise. On having this experience, the Zen master Hakuin said, "After this, seeing things of the world is like seeing the back of my own hand." Zen proposes to do this through controlling and purifying the mind — cleaning out the Eighth Consciousness, the Alaya Vijnana. (Alaya means "receptacle," as in Himalaya, receptacle of snow. Vijnana is "consciousness.") This usually takes long and arduous work, often to the exclusion of other things, as the mind becomes one-pointed through such discipline as the Koan practice. T'ai Chi Chih works from the other end, not from Mind but from the Chi, which affects the Mind, just as the Mind affects the Chi. But T'ai Chi Chih also affects the health, through circulation and balancing of the Chi — this is the great bonus. It does not require giving up anything. I wish I could get Zen monks and Masters to do T'ai Chi Chih; most of those I know suffer stomach ailments from poor, soft food and from long periods of sitting without compensating periods of stimulating the Chi ("Ki" in Japanese, "Prana" in Sanskrit). So you can reach the same result through difficult mind control in Zen or through easy T'ai Chi Chih practice working with the Chi. This is possible because of the reciprocal relationship of Mind and Chi, a little-known fact of great importance.

Cosmic Rhythm

It is interesting to speculate about Cosmic Rhythm. Although Buddhism says all effects come from causes (there being no First Cause), many events seem the result of cyclic, not causal, influences. The plum blossom pushes through the snow in February in Japan, and the sun comes up at a predictable time each day, bringing cyclical daytime after cyclical night. There is no way the plum blossom can know when it is time to emerge; certainly the late winter weather isn't any warmer. Such events as these are part of a natural Cosmic Rhythm. Many have thought how wonderful it would be if they could accord with this Cosmic Rhythm. The Chinese speak of moving with the Tao. And that's where T'ai Chi Chih comes in. The steady practice of T'ai Chi Chih — and, if desired, of the greatly stepped-up Seijaku — offers an easy way to enter this flow. And when we arrive at the point where no one is doing T'ai Chi Chih, where T'ai Chi Chih is doing T'ai Chi Chih, that is letting the Tao play us. All that's needed is sincerity and perseverance; too much self-clinging will make both these difficult.

To know the Cosmic Principle by entering the Cosmic Rhythm — Ah!

A Spiritual Life in a Materialistic World

When I gave an evening course of this nature at the Monterey Peninsula College, I was amazed by the amount of interest it developed. Apparently people are not only concerned about making a living, developing meaningful relationships and coping with the inevitability of death, but they also want to learn how to live their lives without hypocrisy. If the boss says to lie, that he or she is not in, don't I have to obey to keep my job? And if I do lie, why do I have a terrible feeling? After hearing a sermon on Sunday, why do I have to break all the rules the following week?

This is all part of finding out "Who" and "What" I am. In order to know "What" I am, I must first find out "Who" I am.

The Lotus Sutra says:

From the State of Emptiness
Man's body is a body pervading the Universe,
Man's voice is a voice filling the Universe,
Man's life is a life without limit.

Sinking into the Essence

It is hard for students, and even teachers, to understand that T'ai Chi Chih is not just a beneficial exercise. It is so obvious that it has great physical benefits, that it helps control weight, and that, without effort or perspiration, it greatly enhances the energy level. The tendency is to feel that these are the major benefits of T'ai Chi Chih practice. If the one practising persists, however, the deeper levels — the Essence of T'ai Chi Chih, if you will — begin to dawn on the practiser and it is realized that T'ai Chi Chih is unique in design and that one begins to sense, and flow with, the great Cosmic Rhythm. T'ai Chi Chih is not designed for self-defense or any form of violence; rather it is an *inner* discipline ("Naikan" in Japanese and "Nei Kung" in Chinese) that brings to life the dormant Vital Force ("Intrinsic Energy") and balances it as it circulates it, breaking down blockages that may have existed for a long time, in a sense offering a rebirth if the student is sincere enough.

Words play no part, nor do concepts. The Prana (Chi) knows well enough what to do without an intellectual road map. All the practiser has to do is enjoy it and reap the benefits of renewed Life Force.

Justin F. Stone ....

Teh — Power of Inner Sincerity

Teh (Inner Sincerity) is the basis of T'ai Chi Chih. It is the power of Inner Sincerity, as exemplified by T'ai Chi Chih teachers, that has been responsible for the rapid growth of T'ai Chi Chih. This type of person who is drawn to T'ai Chi Chih, and wants to become a teacher, is almost always a deeply sincere person, eager to pass on the benefits he or she has gained from T'ai Chi Chih practice. So often I get letters from new teachers saying, "T'ai Chi Chih has changed my life. Thank you, thank you. I am eager to help others gain the same benefits from the discipline you originated." This is more rewarding than any riches I might have gained from T'ai Chi Chih. There isn't the slightest doubt in my mind of the future of T'ai Chi Chih; there are reasons why it is here, and there are reasons why you, the teacher, have been brought to it. It is not by accident that you are teaching T'ai Chi Chih, and you have a responsibility to keep the practice pure and to be completely honest in your dealings with students.

Emotionalism and sentimentality have little use in the practice of the discipline. My own consideration has always been for the welfare of the teachers, not my own, because I feel deeply the power of the teachers' Teh. It is our jewel, and I fully expect this great power to bring T'ai Chi Chih to deserving people all over the planet. Never underrate T'ai Chi Chih or feel that it exists only for our own benefit.

I congratulate you on being a T'ai Chi Chih teacher! Please never stop trying to improve your practice; this is part of the responsibility of being a teacher.

Note: T'ai Chi Chih should not be thought of as exercise. Exercise implies effort, and effort is counterproductive in T'ai Chi Chih. It must be done softly with the "effort of no effort"

110

to be most effective. Sincere teachers, who practise a good deal themselves, gradually come to realize the true way of movement in T'ai Chi Chih. Those who give careless interviews in which T'ai Chi Chih is cited as "exercise" are doing harm to T'ai Chi Chih. The purpose of T'ai Chi Chih is to circulate and balance the Chi, and to do this, movement must be from the center of the body, not from the shoulders and arms. "How to move" is the most important point of T'ai Chi Chih. ■

A Visit

When someone comes to visit me
I take my cue from him or her.
If he speaks in a transcendental manner
We dwell in Emptiness.
Should he speak from Prajna Wisdom,
The flow will be smooth.
I am not here to preach or correct;

Offer gold and I will give back gems.
Linger in the dust
And we will speak in banal terms.
It rests with you, my friend.

Yoga

There are many forms of Yoga in India — most are not known or practised in the West. Jnana Yoga (the Yoga of discrimination, as with Shankara and Ramana Maharshi) and Raja Yoga (the Kingly Yoga of eight sections) require long years of training from a true Guru, whereas the little bit of Hatha Yoga (Sun-Moon Yoga, one of five preliminaries of Raja Yoga) that is taught in the West is often taught by inexperienced teachers after a few weeks of training, thereby increasing very real dangers.

I have heard westerners say they teach Raja Yoga, but when I ask if they instruct in Pratyahara (fifth of the preliminaries) and insist on Yama (for social development) and Niyama (for personal development) for their students, they don't know what I'm talking about. Actually, I do not know any western teacher who knows how to teach Pratyahara (the withdrawing of the senses from the field of the senses, thereby immunizing the Yogi from pain), though a few may bluff and call it "interiorization," an abstract, general term.

Quite a few of the Yogis I lived with in the Himalayan foothills practised forms roughly subsumed under "Kundalini Yoga," and I saw one, without a teacher, who went out of his mind. Meditation or Mantra Yoga was almost always a necessity for their practice. They generally followed sadhanas given them by their gurus.

Those doing Mantra Yoga were given their mantra in initiation by their teachers. Only a recognized Yogic Master, usually of a particular tradition, has the right to give such initiation — this is a must — and it carries on the teaching and tradition of the originator. True Gurus are even stricter than Zen Masters, and one does what he or she is told or is sent packing. I saw it happen in the Himalayas, and a rather tragic

112

man, who had been a successful lawyer in Lucknow before becoming a Yogi, was thrown out of an Ashram with no place to go. I gave him the small amount of money necessary to take a bus to Dehra Dun (where he might pick up a patron who would place him in another Ashram), but I have no way of knowing how his life turned out. He was never meant to be a Yogi, but gave his estate to his family when he reached the age of 50 and tried to follow the ancient scriptures in retiring from the world.

Those who initiate or pose without the right to do so are incurring serious Karmic debts. Although I was initiated into one of the great traditions of India, and asked to work for them in that country, I have no right to initiate or give a mantra. There are dangers inherent in various Yogas and the seeker must be careful to be led by those competent to do so. As is true with Martial Arts, it takes many, many years of untiring labor to be ready to be a Yoga teacher.

Three Little Words

Vairagya, Ahimsa, Prajna. There! I've put the whole of Spiritual Practice into three Sanskrit words, meaning, respectively: Non-Attachment (or Detachment), Non-Violence (in all forms, not only physical) and Inherent Wisdom. Living from natural, intuitive Inherent Wisdom is the reward for successful practice.

And the aim of all true Spiritual Practice (having nothing to do with Religious Dogma and Mythology) is to eliminate the Habit Energies (Vashanas) that have accumulated through many lifetimes, purging the compulsions that have formed us and have guided our lives, making our Karma.

Ahimsa, non-violence, is comparatively easy. Vairagya, detachment, is terribly difficult in our modern life, being in the midst of it and yet detached from it. Not one in a million realizes Vairagya.

Live a straightforward, non-scheming life and you will be on the way. ■

▼ ▼ ▼ ▼ ▼ ▼

You can never understand "Life" from the personal standpoint, saying: "I was put here for some reason and I should have satisfaction and meaning in my life." The realized ones speak from the impersonal; their conversation is not ego centered. When you do T'ai Chi Chih and feel the flow of the Chi, you are in accord with the Real. What is there to understand?

114

Spiritual and Physical Purification

All organisms are in a constant state of purification — both spiritually and physically. Physically, the activity to throw off impurities brings on what we call "illness." To put chemicals in the body (pain-killers, sleeping pills, etc.) simply adds to the impurities to be thrown off and builds up the need for subsequent purification.

Spiritually, there is evolvement. Karma (the result of habit-energies, *Vashanas*, and tendencies, *Samskaras*) causes us to have experiences that will hasten evolution or purifying of the Chi (Prana). When we do such practices as T'ai Chi Chih we are aiding this process.

The above is true, but only at one level. At the deepest, non-dualistic level it is not apparent. ■

▼ ▼ ▼ ▼ ▼ ▼

Paul Reps, asked what he believed in, answered: "Nothing. If I believed in anything, there would be two." This is one side of the matter.

Teaching Tips for T'ai Chi Chih Teachers
(also useful for students)

A good T'ai Chi Chih teacher must be able to detect the faults of the student — and then be able to correct them. This means that, through his or her own practice, the teacher must have come to more than a shallow understanding of T'ai Chi Chih movements. Teaching is more than just showing where to place the hands and feet.

Once the teacher has shown the correct way to move (softly, with continuity), he or she might look for faults in balance. In a movement such as "Pulling Taffy," the pupil may have shifted the weight to the left side while the hands are still on the right side. (The hands and weight must shift together to the Yang side.) This is awkward. As in all movements, the shift in body weight must be synchronized with the movement of the hands. Teachers must have an understanding of "substantial" and "insubstantial."

If the pupil does not have enough body coordination to do this, then he or she must be allowed to do the best he or she can. However, a teacher must be able to do this gradual shift of weight correctly. The pupil will imitate what and how the movement is done by the teacher.

With most it is a lack of understanding, and the teacher must be able to spot the difficulty and correct it through example.

Another common difficulty is moving forward to a stiff front knee, instead of a bent knee that takes the weight and becomes substantial. This can also happen in regard to the back knee. The back knee should bend the same amount as the front knee, not one bending and the other becoming stiff (and remaining insubstantial).

116

With almost every movement, there are things to look for that need to be corrected, and the teacher must realize this. ∎

▼ ▼ ▼ ▼ ▼ ▼

You cannot give the same teaching to two people. It must fit the Karma of each one and never be a teaching by rote. How do you know what teaching to give? You will be guided.

Our Very Nature

Most students come to T'ai Chi Chih feeling, "I am going to do a beneficial exercise." Eventually they find it *is* beneficial — and joyous — but they still think of it as exercise, and still put the "I" in there. As they proceed farther, they begin to slowly realize the Essence of T'ai Chi Chih and one day they have the experience that "no one is doing T'ai Chi Chih. T'ai Chi Chih is doing T'ai Chi Chih." Now they have the "I" out of the way. Their practice is done without thought, concentrating on the soles of the feet. This "non-ego" state is greatly beneficial; it is what makes T'ai Chi Chih more than exercise and has a deeply spiritual benefit. One does not have to outguess T'ai Chi Chih, nor to understand it intellectually (having to do with the circulation and balancing of the Vital Force, and the benefits thereby realized). At this point the practice has become meditation, and the practiser is gaining the considerable physical benefits while evolving spiritually. It is so easy to learn and easy to do, yet look at the extent of the rewards!

To get to the point where one realizes the Essence of T'ai Chi Chih is wonderful. As I have pointed out many times, Bliss is our very nature, and here is a simple way to realize that Bliss. The habit energies do not at all intrude on the practice of the movements, and there is no effort made (though some do make the mistake of trying hard). If one needs a goal, why not aim at realizing the Essence of T'ai Chi Chih? It is worth the no-effort effort.

Ritual

I had a good friend who asked me, many years ago, "Perhaps we should all belong to the Church of Rome." I asked him why, and he answered that it had dogma, doctrine, tradition and extensive Ritual. I asked him if he was more interested in Ritual than in finding out "who" and "what" he was. Surprised, he asked, "How do you do that?" I answered that it was the purpose of Zen practice, and also of Yoga. It gave him something to think about. Ritual makes us feel secure, in sharing some action with others; it does not help us to know ourselves in the largest sense.

Meditation and Concentration

"Concentration" and "meditation" are two, but they are often linked together under the heading "Meditation." Concentration is intense focus on an object, often until one becomes the object and the mind is one-pointed. "Zazen" in Zen is like this, as is the practice of the T'ien T'ai ("Tendai" in Japan). Koan practice, in Zen, brings about a one-pointed mind, which sometimes leads to an enlightenment experience.

"Meditation," in its deepest sense brings about a focused mind that becomes "no-pointed." Using a Zen term, this is "Mu Shin" in its true sense. When one comes out of the deep immersion that true meditation brings, one has to consciously rebuild the world. It has a deep and lasting effect.

We have the ocean, and the waves that arise from it, looking like this:

The waves rise and fall, creating quite a commotion, though the waves that arise are merely a manifestation of the ocean itself; there is no difference between them. If we can sink *between* the waves, to the ocean's unruffled surface, we have peace with no change.

Similarly, there is the mind, from which thoughts arise, looking like this:

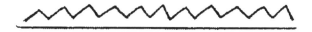

If we can detect the space *before* thought, the space between thoughts, we can sink between the whirling thoughts to the absolute quiet of the mind without thought, called in India the "Turiya" level, or fourth state of consciousness. The first three — the waking, sleeping, and dreaming states — are like the "unreal" movie that is projected on the permanent, unchanging screen. All emotions and upheavals occur in the first three states, but the reality is the fourth, unchanging one. This is represented by the incessant droning sound, beneath the lightning changes that occur in the solo instruments, representing the ever-present reality. My teaching of meditation is primarily aimed at realizing, and resting in, this underlying state.

To rest in this Turiya state is to realize, and manifest, Samadhi. In Yoga this is the ultimate goal, though Zen, and Buddhism in general, want to go on to "Prajna," the inherent wisdom. It is through the practice of this Samadhi that the Prajna, latent in all, is uncovered.

I have been with Yogis as they practise and realize the Bliss of this Samadhi (Turiya state). Many have developed strong powers that they could use profitably in the world, but why would they want to? To be able to enter this fourth state at will brings the greatest Bliss, and probably satisfaction, that can be known in this world — not to mention the effect it has on future lives. Can we live the usual everyday life in the world and still realize this Blissful awakening? This is a difficult question to answer. Those that I have known who have realized it (not the fulfillment of some transitional goal) have always been those who have given up everything else. Sad, but true, Vairagya (non-attachment) is the absolute necessity. However, we can practise meditation as a portion of our busy lives.

Samatha-Vipasyana
(Holding Fast and Letting Go)

T'ien t'ai Buddhism (Tendai in Japanese) uses "Holding Fast and Letting Go" in their simple but profound meditation, as those who have taken Meditation Retreats with me know. The purpose, of course, is to stop the conceptualizing mind, and prevent the paralyzing Habit Energies that govern our lives. T'ien t'ai has found that such meditation contributes a good deal to healing activities. Many of the T'ien t'ai teachers also discuss the philosophical aspects of this activity.

Zen Buddhism, in its practical way, uses the holding fast and letting go in dealing with serious students and aspirants. I have seen Zen Masters using this technique very effectively. Unexpectedly, they may go along with the thought patterns of the monk or student, then suddenly stop "letting go" in order to pull the rug out from under the conceptualizer's feet ("holding fast"). This can be very painful. Particularly with scholars, who deal in concepts, does this shake the very foundation of thinking — which is what the teacher is aiming for. Only serious aspirants will stand still for this; most feel affronted and lose their urge for "enlightenment." If one is not serious to the point of being willing to accept great change, one should not practice true Zen.

One time I took a Latvian lady to see a Zen Master who was in this country. In typical sentimental (emotional) style she asked why there were different nationalities, why they fought and made wars. He answered by holding up his hand and spreading five fingers. "Why do I have five fingers?" he asked. I rushed over to count his five fingers, and, sure enough, there were five!

After the meeting, the Latvian lady asked me, "Why didn't he answer my question?"

"He gave you the only possible answer," I replied. Holding fast had not agreed with her; she wanted some sort of useless conceptual answer. Few will understand this. ■

▼ ▼ ▼ ▼ ▼ ▼

The important thing about a problem is to understand the ground from which it arose.

About Breathing Techniques

Special breathing techniques should not be applied to T'ai Chi Chih. I have often answered the question about this matter, and have written about it. If you, the teacher, urge special breathing techniques (not natural breathing), you are running the risk of one day facing a lawsuit. They can alter the rhythm of the heart, as I have found out from experience.

It is natural to breathe out as you push forward in "Push Pull," and it is natural to breathe in as you raise the arms in "Rocking Motion," breathing out as you lower them. This is natural and is not what I'm talking about. Again, I repeat, there are no special breathing techniques for T'ai Chi Chih. I am not interested in what goes on in martial arts. I am writing this for protection of the teachers. I want to add that only Master Yogis, who know the dangers, should teach breathing techniques.

Wisdom and Consciousness

To differentiate "Wisdom" (Prajna) and "Consciousness" (Vijnana or Chit) is difficult. When the mind is obscured by habitual thoughts, it may be referred to as "Consciousness." When the obscuring habitual notions are dispersed, it can be called "Prajna" or "Inherent Wisdom."

Acting from Prajna is natural and constructive. Because Zen teachers want students and monks to react spontaneously, they stress Prajna. Acting from ordinary obscured Consciousness can bring suffering.

When Prajna (inherent wisdom) operates, we can understand:

From the State of Emptiness
Man's body is a body filling the Universe,
Man's voice is a voice pervading the Universe,
Man's life is a life without limit. (Lotus Sutra)

When one lies, tells half-truths or rationalizes for self-enhancement, this completely obscures the Prajna. Such a person cannot expect to act from Prajna or live a spiritual life. Particularly is this so when one lies to oneself about motives and actions. Hui Neng stressed that one must have a "straight-forward mind," and this is not easy when it conflicts with ambition or desire. Self-discipline demands that we see things as they are, not the way we want them to be or the way they appear to deluded thinking.

125

The Teacher-Pupil Relationship

The relationship between teacher and pupil is a very noble one in the history of Spiritual Practice. Never, in the history of such relationships, had I ever heard of a chela (or monk, or student) telling, or writing, his Master that "I know more than you do; I have gone past you." It would have been unthinkable. Occasionally a Zen Master, such as Huang Po, might say to his great disciple Lin Chi (known as Rinzai in Japan), "One day your view will surpass mine and you will cut off the heads of all the sages in the world." Notice that it was the *teacher* who made the statement. If a student had made it, it certainly would have alerted the teacher to how far the student still had to go. In many cases, arrogance like this would not have been tolerated.

Trust is the basis of such teacher-pupil relationships. It usually was the stern teacher who was later recalled with love by the enlightened pupil. If a Master is kind to a monk, a pupil or a chela, it means he or she is hopeless. The more outstanding the pupil, the harder the discipline. It is said that, in early days of India, penalties for a transgression were more severe for a high caste person than for a low-caste (or casteless) one. It was felt that the high-caste, educated one should know better. So a Master could probably be accused of picking on his best pupil, as he demanded the most from him. Abbot Oboro of the Soto Zen sect complained, while he was a monk, "Why doesn't he let up on me for just a second?" Then, when his teacher died, he felt an "unutterable loneliness." He knew that, now he was a respected Abbot, nobody would ever speak to him like that again.

A good teacher is one who repeats and repeats, and emphasizes sternly what the pupil seems to be ignoring. Ask a Japanese student who has studied flower arranging or tea

126

ceremony! "Kibishi Sensei" is a strict teacher, and much honored by the Japanese people. Many years ago one of the certified teachers got a job teaching T'ai Chi Chih at a small college near his home town. At the end of the first term, evaluation papers (for the opinions of students) were handed out. I feel these are destructive; the pupil cannot always understand the teacher, and this man was an excellent teacher. Having taught T'ai Chi Ch'uan, the movements came easily to him and he really knew how to move. His was not the shallow understanding at which some teachers stop.

On several of the evaluation papers, students had written that they did not like his blackboard technique. Big deal! A stern teacher, he had been working hard to teach them T'ai Chi Chih, not handwriting skills. Because of these evaluations the teacher was not rehired. This devastated him, and he and his wife drove sixty miles to see me.

"Do you think my husband is a good teacher?" she asked as soon as they arrived. "He's an excellent teacher, " I replied. "He really understands the Yin-Yang relationship."

"They, why did they fire him?" she demanded.

"Oh, if he had had a few beers with the students, cracked some jokes (not his personality), or done a tap dance, perhaps he would have been popular," I replied. That teacher never taught T'ai Chi Chih again, and it's our loss.

The breech of a teacher-pupil relationship is a serious Karmic matter. As the teacher is usually quite a bit older (and, sometimes, infirm), respect and consideration is all important. Chinese Zen monks would rather die than hurt a teacher.

I think I've belabored my point. Shallow pupils usually withdraw from a strict teacher. Serious ones welcome the help he or she can give.

127

Discipline

There are some lazy people who do not want to take the trouble to do something properly and therefore invent rationalizations for not making the effort, usually using generalities such as "love," "freedom," etc., which are meaningless unless they are lived. When I was learning Japanese, a man from Japan said to me, "If you are going to speak the language, learn to speak it properly." This made a big impression on me. If you are going to become a doctor, you must pass medical exams and learn to do the procedures correctly. If you want to play a Mozart Sonata, or sing a Mozart opera, I suggest you follow the marks that Mozart wrote. People will differ in the way they sound because of the difference in capabilities, but they will all be playing or singing the notes Mozart wrote. I have never heard of an undisciplined opera singer, or a lazy concert pianist. Similarly, if you want to teach T'ai Chi Chih, you must first do it correctly yourself or it becomes a sham. Teh — inner sincerity — demands that you practice what you preach. The Japanese monk, Senzaki, said, "It is better to discipline ourselves than to have life do it for us." Those who drift aimlessly might take note of this remark.

Nature of Chi

At a recent T'ai Chi Chih meeting in the Albuquerque Center, I mentioned several sentences to give an insight into the truth of TCC and to motivate those who practise it. I was asked to make these available to readers. Of course, they could become whole paragraphs; they are from ancient Chinese writings, as follows:

"It is Chi that determines human mental and physical conditions. The way in which Chi is expressed is commonly known as the nature of things."

"Chi is the origin of our life energy; in other words, our life is determined by Chi."

"Chi is not an element of any kind, but, rather, it is the origin of everything."

"Since Chi is the ultimate energy from which the universe and the essence of all existence is derived, Chi is immune to the limitations of time and space."■

129

The hand of Satori is held out.

Too few can be too many.

The ocean waves: the essence is water.

The Japanese poet and artist, Nobutada, wrote, "Quietness and Emptiness are enough to pass through life without error" (or suffering, I might add).

Note this, you who are always rushing and being emotionally stirred by every phenomenon.

Let Go!

The idea of attaining enlightenment by trying harder has always seemed to me to be ludicrous. Realizing enlightenment is not a matter of making a breakthrough, after great effort, and finding something new; it's simply a matter of recognizing what is. Yet Zen teachers continually implore their monks or students to "try harder." My teacher told me to "take this more seriously," though the objective is to banish the Vashanas (habit energies), not make new ones — in Buddhist terms, to clean out the eighth consciousness, the "Alaya Vijnana" (Receptacle of Consciousness).

Similarly, in T'ai Chi Chih, the most important thing is "softness," the "effort of no effort." This isn't accomplished by trying hard but by "letting go." Trying hard implies effort, great effort, but we are not exercising in doing T'ai Chi Chih, we are swimming through very heavy air without effort.

Enlightenment is not the product of dualistic thinking; its very nature is unity. This is beyond the power of ordinary conceptual thinking. It means letting go of habitual patterns of thought; if necessary, stopping thinking. Patanjali, called "the Father of Yoga," gave as his first aphorism the "suppression of mental modification." This can hardly be accomplished by forming new modifications.

In conclusion, to achieve enlightenment, to practise T'ai Chi Chih (these can be the same) LET GO!

131

How our Lives are Built

In speaking or writing about Vashanas, it is easy to give the impression that they are something "bad." Actually, these "habit energies" are neither good nor bad. It is impossible to live everyday life without building such habit energies. You would not be able to drive a car, play a piano, or cook a meal without having formed a pattern for performing these acts. Only a monk or a recluse can noticeably cut down the making of Vashanas and the eventual tendencies (Samskaras) that come from them. Patanjali, called the "Father of Yoga," said that Yoga Practice was "Chit Vriti Narodha," suppression of mental modifications. These mental modifications, called "Vritti," are what dictate our lives, indeed, form us.

To live a life in which the making of mental modifications is attenuated or suppressed is impossible in ordinary life. Only the one determined to make the spiritual progress necessary to assure better lives in the future, with "Moksha" (Salvation) being the eventual goal, can live the kind of life necessary for progress, giving up all possibility of Greed, Anger and Delusion. And this includes the Greed for Life.

It is not difficult to see how these Vashanas form our Karma, or, rather, the Fruits of our Karma. "Karma" means "action," though not in the ordinary sense, and we reap the fruit of our actions (the motive being all-important). We can control our future by being careful of the Karma we build.

This is not an easy subject for people with only superficial interest to understand, but it, obviously, is the most important matter in the world. We are all born and we all die; this is inevitable. But how, in what state, are we born again? Remember, your future lies in your own hands. Recently I counseled a former student of mine, "In this life, do what is right, not what you think you can get away with." Sounds like preaching, doesn't it? Yet, in light of what is written above, it is necessary to add it for the good of all. ■

▼ ▼ ▼ ▼ ▼ ▼

Confucius stressed "human-heartedness" and "Teh." I find them preferable to the attitude of the Zen Master who turned his back on all callers.

How We Live

People do their thinking with their emotions. This is a sure path to suffering. They manifest hate while speaking abstractly of love. Then they wonder why they have unfulfilled lives.

The Buddhist Abidhamma (Buddhist psychology) says there are sixty-odd joyous states of consciousness and only three miserable ones. Yet people rush blindly toward the three negative ways. Why? If we know that craving, anger, and delusion cause us suffering, why do we entertain these three? Are we compulsive and compelled to think and act in this manner?

In order to hide the truth from ourselves, we cultivate neuroses. "He went to his Mahasamadhi" we say, when the truth is, "He died." Aren't we all going to die?

Spiritual practice causes us to accord with death, not to fear it. We know excess attachment and aversion (I love this, I hate that) cause us suffering, yet we allow sentiment and deluded emotion to lead us down that path. "Impermanence" is a fact of life; why fear it? Tantra says that every cell in the body can be brought to a point of ecstasy. Inside we have the treasure we are searching for. Why not follow this joyous way?

One Mind

If one seeks enlightenment apart from the things of the world, that is mistaken. In truth, there is only enlightenment. Properly understood, even ignorance is enlightenment.

One time, living at an Ashram in America, a very fine nun spoke to me and said, "When I go down into the world to buy groceries, I can't wait to get back to this sanctuary." I answered that, unfortunately, she did not understand what she had been taught. Not by seeking escape from the world would she attain understanding. She was a' very dedicated and faithful practitioner of the Ramakrishna teaching, yet she suffered from this delusion.

For those on a path, or those who are true seekers, I have a question. In Zen it is said that there is nothing but this one Mind (which is no mind). Accordingly, I ask, "Does this one Mind manifest Consciousness, or does Consciousness manifest this one Mind?" This type of inquiry is not a waste of time, nor is it an intellectual exercise. It is a good way to arouse intuition of the Truth.

The Self of All Things

The great Indian Sage, Ramana Maharshi, told his followers to ask themselves the question, "Who Am I?" A psychiatrist or psychoanalyst might also want to know the answer to that question, but the purpose of these two people is widely different from what Ramana Maharshi had in mind. Actually, they are at opposite ends of the pole.

The "I" that the psychiatrist and psychoanalyst had in mind was the little personality, the identity with a name that functions in the world. The doctor wants to know how this person handles the problems of the world, and determines to strengthen the patient's ego-center so that he or she can cope with the vicissitudes of life, everyday life. Ramana Maharshi, on the other hand, had a much bigger aim in mind. This "I" he wanted you to discover was nothing other than the Eternal Center. He wanted you to be One with all things, the Self of all things.

This misunderstanding is one of the great hindrances in Spiritual Training, which is not aimed at having you make more money or building a better relationship with your spouse. If you want to know Truth (or, better yet, live it), you will not receive answers by analyzing why your boss fired you unexpectedly. To function in the world it may be necessary for you to understand your own shortcomings and correct them, but that has nothing to do with making spiritual progress. The Becoming that eventually can lead you back to where you, in truth, have always been is a puzzle. When Paul Reps said, "Ah, but if you had not been on the Spiritual Path for thirty-five years you would have never known there is Nothing To Be Done," he was expressing the answer to the problem of Being and Becoming.

Buddhism says there are three facts of life: 1) Anica (Impermanence), 2) Dukkha (Suffering), and 3) An-Atman (no permanent self or identity). The Dukkha here can be interpreted as the suffering that comes from being separated from your true self, not merely the pain that occurs in daily life. Until you know Who and What you are, it is hard to be content.

The "Who Am I?" of Ramana Maharshi can lead you to knowing what is said in the Lotus Sutra:

From the State of Emptiness
Man's body is a body pervading the Universe,
Man's voice is a voice filling the Universe
Man's life is a life without limit. ▪

▼ ▼ ▼ ▼ ▼ ▼

The moment of Enlightenment, concluded Zen Master Takuan, is the understanding of unity with all creation, in which there is no need for individual desires.

137

Spiritual Progress

To realize Spiritual Progress, the "pleasure principle" must be attenuated. Why make spiritual progress? Because it is the only way to Joy.

The one with low spiritual consciousness, small awareness, is never content. There is constant suffering, based on the fact that everything is judged from the basis of "I." Universal Consciousness is not dreamed of. The statement of Zen Master Hakuin, "After this (enlightenment), seeing things of the world is like seeing the back of my own hand," is incomprehensible.

Where there is an artificial "high," there is always an artificial "low;" only True Joy, which is not the result of some action, is different.

My meditation students are asked to detect what is prior to thought, to rest in the still ocean below the waves. Then real Bliss can be attained. It cannot be gained through worldly activities. Hence the statement: "To realize Spiritual Progress, the pleasure principle must be attenuated."

Removing those Clouds...

"Enlightenment" is a strange word. It can mean the "Satori" Experience of Zen, where extreme concentration can force a powerful experience, perhaps before the student is ready for it. It can mean the "Moksha" state of India, where the "Jivan Mukta" (enlightened or freed in this lifetime) has escaped the wheel of birth and death.

In truth, is there such a thing as an "unenlightened" person? All the factors of enlightenment are present. The "Vashanas" (habit energies) and "Samskaras" (tendencies) cover them up — that is all. The sun does not cease to shine because clouds obscure it. Think about that. No one lacks any thing, though it is not perceived that way. All beings are possessed of the same life force.

Those who study T'ai Chi Chih, practise it, and then let it fall by the wayside will not allow the wind to blow the clouds away.

Justin F. Stone ....

Deep Study

If you will go and live with a great Yogic teacher, you will find that being is equivalent to consciousness. Since consciousness implies duality, this means there is something besides consciousness (awareness). Man is being (he thinks of himself as "a being") and being is defined as Sat Chit Ananda — "Being Consciousness Bliss." This implies that the very nature of being — and, therefore, of man — is bliss (Ananda in Sanskrit). Through "becoming" man attains to this bliss, which is his true nature. However, at a lower level, the Indian Sages have said that man is predominantly one of three states (gunas): the pure Sattvic state, the active Rajasic state, or the clouded-over, dull Tamasic state. If we are born with the third, the lethargic, fearful state of Tamas, there is little we can do to attain bliss. We can work to better our makeup so we can attain to bliss in another lifetime, but, the problem is, our lethargic, fearful nature will prevent us from doing so. To move up the ladder is rare. How many have the will to do so? How many will realize his or her own dullness?

An ancient saying is "As above so below." All that exists in the macrocosm exists, potentially, within man, the microcosm. In truth, we are Divinity, but that blessed state is covered by clouds of ignorance. Avidya (ignorance — literally "not seeing") is the cause of our troubles. Buddhism has said that there are over sixty states of mind, but we tend to stick to the three that bring us suffering: Greed (the desire to possess, covetousness), Anger (envy, etc.) and Delusion (brought about by the tendencies that have developed by our habit-energies, or Vashanas). The conceit that sometimes comes from a little spiritual study makes any progress impossible.

When we live at a good Ashram in India, faithful practice
gives us an opportunity to first experience this bliss, which is
not satisfaction of desire. Then there is the danger that it
makes everything else look insipid and we get stuck in the
"Vertical," the sense of oneness that keeps us from the world
and from fulfilling our Karma. This is why Zen speaks of
"climbing a hundred-foot pole" and then going on from there,
which, strangely enough, means descending from the exclusive
state of oneness to live in the everyday world again (and to
help others).

Teilhard de Chardin says that religion is "the search for
ultimates." This has nothing to do with dogma, doctrine, or
institutional religion. How many people are interested in a
search for ultimates, or even ask the question, "Why are we
here?" Shallow character, complete concentration on daily
problems of life and desire for sense gratification — including
the need for entertainment and diversion — keep the average
person from even coming to grip with the certainty that he or
she will die — this being the one certainty. The search for
security is hopeless: there is none. All philosophic search is
meant just to bring us face to face with uncertainty and to
accord with impermanence, not easy to do. To go deep within,
far beyond thought, is the one way we have of getting answers
or annulling questions. Usually, a true spiritual guide is
necessary, but he or she cannot remake the gunas with which
we are born or drastically change our Karma (more accu-
rately, the fruits of our Karma). We will find our way,
however, if we are sincere and really want to. It is helpful to
remember that man's real nature is bliss.

For a complete catalog of books and tapes by Justin F. Stone and other authors, please contact:

Good Karma Publishing, Inc.
P.O. Box 511
Fort Yates, ND 58538
Phone - 701/854-7459
Fax - 701/854-2004